MEMOIR

OF

CAPTAIN DALTON

MEMOIR

OF

CAPTAIN DALTON,

H.E.I.C.S.

DEFENDER OF TRICHINOPOLY, 1752-1753.

CHARLES DALTON, F.R.G.S.

GYAN

Published by

GYAN

Gyan Publishing House
5, Ansari Road
Daryaganj, New Delhi-110002
Phone: 011-47034999, 9811692060
E-mail: books@gyanbooks.com

Distribution Network
gyanbooks.com
India, USA, Canada, UK, Australia, France

ISBN : 978-81-212-9504-8 (PB)
First Published, 1886

2nd Impression 2023

Printed at: Gyan Press, Delhi.

MEMOIR OF CAPTAIN DALTON
Author: CHARLES DALTON

MEMOIR

OF

CAPTAIN DALTON,

H.E.I.C.S.

DEFENDER OF TRICHINOPOLY, 1752–1753.

BY

CHARLES DALTON, F.R.G.S.,

AUTHOR OF "LIFE AND TIMES OF GENERAL SIR EDWARD CECIL."

"A gallant and able officer."

MALCOLM'S *Life of Clive*, i. 119.

1886.

CAPTAIN JOHN DALTON.

FROM THE ORIGINAL PORTRAIT, BY ROMNEY,

AT LANGTON HALL, MALTON.

IN AFFECTIONATE MEMORY

OF

MY BELOVED AUNT AND FRIEND,

ISABELLA DALTON.

PREFACE.

"Facts are stubborn things."

THE memoirs now offered to the reading public were written some years ago, and a few copies printed for private circulation. A revised edition of these memoirs is now made public, because I find that few, if any, outside the immediate circle of Captain Dalton's descendants, are aware that Robert Orme, the Indian historian of the eighteenth century, transferred a great part of the contents of the MS. journal kept by Captain Dalton, during the last few years of his service in India, to his *History of the War in India*, which appeared in 1763. Much of the credit that devolved upon Orme for his historical production was really due to Dalton, and it is because this fact still remains unknown that I now publish the military memoirs of my great-grandfather, who supplied the historian with the minute details which characterise a great part of the first volume of a work which went through four editions, and has supplied the foundation-stone of all subsequent works relating to the transactions of the British in India a hundred and thirty odd years ago.

I have no wish to detract from the fame of the mighty dead. I merely wish to do an act of justice to the memory of a brave and single-minded soldier, who, I am quite sure, desired no public acknowledgment of the favour he conferred upon the historian, by furnishing him with the interesting chronicle of the stirring military events which took place in Southern India between 1750 and 1754.

Succeeding generations of biographers have expressed their admiration of Orme's historical powers. Here are two specimens :—

"Few historians," says Chalmers, "have connected the events of their story with more perspicuity or related them with more conciseness."

"Orme, inferior to no English historian," wrote Lord Macaulay, "in style and power of painting, is minute even to tediousness. In one volume he allots on an average a closely printed quarto page to the events of every forty-eight hours."

The lynx-eyed Macaulay saw, what other biographers failed to discover, the discrepancy in style in parts of the Indian historian's work. Had he known, what the reader now does, that Orme had fitted in whole extracts from Captain Dalton's Indian journal into his "History," weaving the whole together with the dexterity and ingenuity of a first-class parlour-fire historian, he would not have wondered at the minuteness, which is more in keeping with a daily journal than a history extending over many years.

Again, Sir John Malcolm, who knew, from Orme's own letters to Clive, that the historian sent his proof-sheets to Lord Clive for correction, and received maps and much valuable information from that great soldier, does not appear to have been aware of the existence of Dalton's Journal, nor of Orme's wholesale extracts from it.

"No apology," writes Malcolm in his *Life of*

Clive, " is necessary for adopting his (Orme's) narrative, which, in its very minuteness, is as interesting as it is instructive."

During the last twelve months of Captain Dalton's residence in India, Orme was absent from that country, having returned to England; Clive was also in England; so that Dalton's journal, recording, as it did, the chief events in Southern India during that stirring year, was peculiarly valuable to a historian. If it be thought unprecedented to disclose the secrets of a historian who has been long dead, I may quote a precisely similar case.

More than 250 years after Holinshed's *Chronicles* appeared in print, a MS. journal relating to the siege of Guisnes, and written by Arthur Lord Grey de Wilton, was discovered in an old box of deeds at Oulton Park, Cheshire, and was found to coincide, nearly verbatim, with the account given of that siege by Holinshed in his *Chronicles of England and Scotland*. Holinshed never mentioned who furnished him with this interesting journal, which he transferred wholesale to his history; and, on account of this silence on his part, a member of the Grey de

Wilton family, in 1847, published, in one of the Camden Society's publications, the newly-discovered journal of his ancestor, penned nearly 300 years before, and gave the parallel passages from Holinshed, showing most clearly how the old chronicler had copied entire passages from the manuscript lent him by Lord Grey de Wilton. Here, if it were wanted, is precedent enough for my showing where Orme gleaned some of his graphic descriptions. But in the case of Captain Dalton's Journal, which contains over 166 folio pages, there would be nothing gained by publishing the entire MS. now, as the pith of it is to be found in Orme's history. I have given, in the following pages, more extracts from Orme's history than from Dalton's journal, as I feel, all the time I am quoting from Orme, that my ancestor supplied the information, although what he wrote in the bustle of camp life, and in the few leisure moments at his disposal, when commandant of the beleaguered town of Trichinopoly, has, in some parts, been pruned down to due historic proportions.

I am much indebted to my brother-in-law, the Rev. C. B. Norcliffe, of Langton Hall, Malton, for the extracts he has kindly copied for me from Captain Dalton's journal—which valuable manuscript is in his possession—as well as for the tracings of the two military plans drawn by Captain Dalton in his journal, and which I have had lithographed, in a reduced size, for my reprint.

I also am much indebted to my cousin Colonel Yule, C.B., Member of the Indian Council, for helping me to obtain access to the East India Records in the India Office, from which records I obtained much valuable information.

Finally, I have to acknowledge, with many thanks, the courtesy and invariable civility I have met with from the officials of the Public Record Office, London, and the Record Office of Ireland in Dublin.

C. DALTON.

32, West Cromwell Road,
London, S.W.

Sept. 15, 1886.

CONTENTS.

CHAPTER VII.

(1751.)

CHAPTER VIII.

(1752.)

CHAPTER IX.

CHAPTER X.

(1752-1753.)

CHAPTER XI.

CHAPTER XII.

(1753-1754.)

CHAPTER XIII.

Plan of Volconda Fort, & the action that happened near it, June 19th 1751.

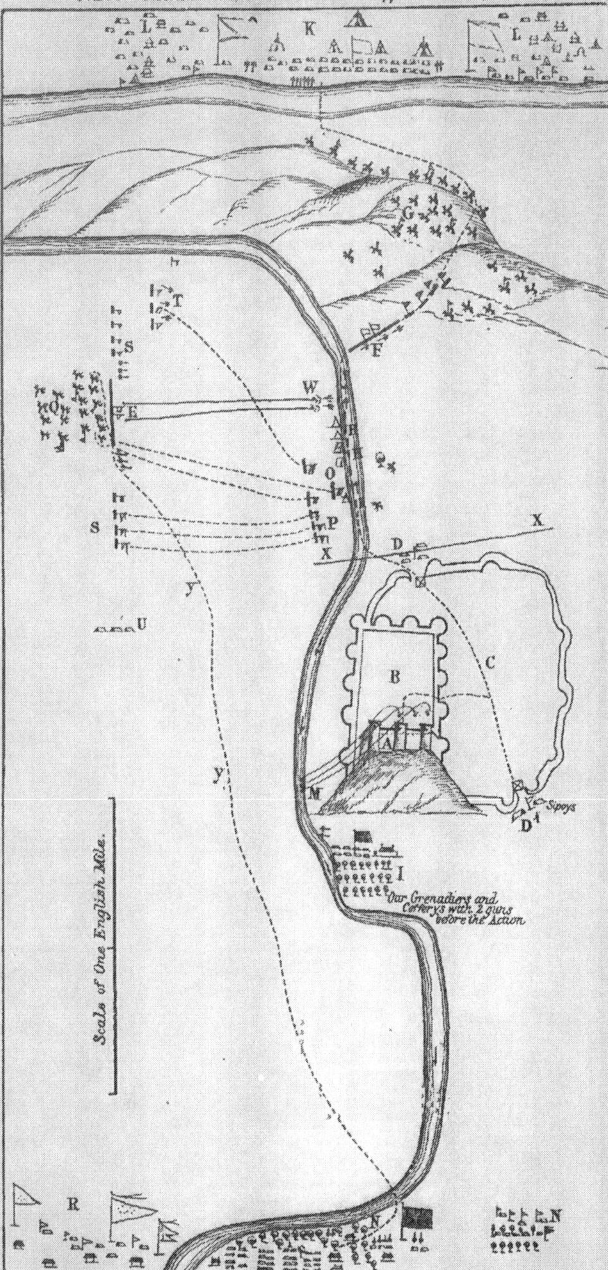

A. Volconda Citadel.
B. The Town.
C. Mud-walled Village.
D. English Guards.
E. English Battalion.
F. French Battalion in march to gain the Water-course.
G. Chunda's Army.
H. Advanced party of the Enemy march.
I. Our advanced Guard before the Action.
K. French Camp.
L. Chunda's Camp.
M. Our Bomb Battery.
N. English Camp.
O. Our Cofferys advancing to stop the Enemy's march.
P. Our Grenadiers and some Sipoys supporting the Cofferys.
Q. Nabob's Horse.
R. His Camp.
S. Sipoys.
T. A Portugue Company and some Sipoys with 3 Guns belonging to the Nabob.
U. Small advanced Party from our Grenadiers before the Action.
W. Two of the Enemy's Guns which made our Battalion retreat while our Coffreys were engaged.
X. Encampment of the Enemy after the Action.
Y. Our Retreat.

Plan of the Action near Wootatoor, July 13th 1751.

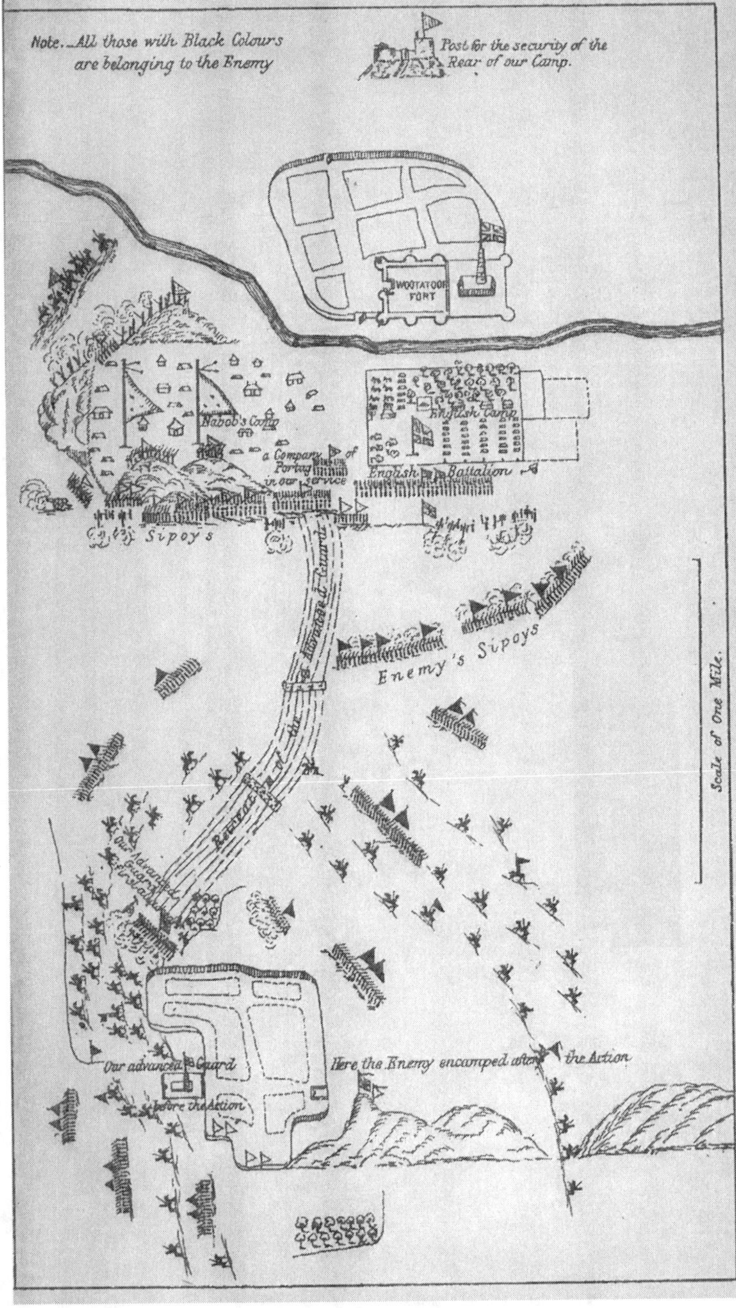

MEMOIR OF CAPTAIN DALTON.

CHAPTER I.

Introduction.—James Dalton appointed to the Sixth Regiment of Foot.—Joins in Dublin.—The Archbishop's Visitation.—The Sixth marches to Limerick, 1719.—Marriage of Lieut. James Dalton.—Birth of John Dalton, 1725.—The Sixth proceeds to Scotland, 1739.—War with Spain.—Ten new Regiments raised.—James Dalton promoted Captain, 1740.—John Dalton obtains a Commission in Hanmer's Marine Regiment, 1741.—The Sixth embarks for West Indies on Active Service.—Death of Captain James Dalton, 1742.—Remarks on the Climate of the West Indies, and of Jamaica in particular.—The Old Marine Regiments.

IN the *Illustrated London News* of September 16, 1854, there is a picture of a new railway bridge across the Cavery, uniting Trichinopoly with the island of Seringham, and the description of Trichinopoly begins as follows :—" Trichinopoly, once the stronghold of British power in Southern India, and rendered famous by the deeds of Clive, Lawrence, Dalton, and other heroes," &c.

The successful defence of Trichinopoly against the French and their allies in 1752–53 by Captain John Dalton, the Commandant, is recorded in every history of British India; but the pleasant task of first making public the memoirs of Captain Dalton's military life, and giving some details of the family of Dalton, has now fallen to my lot.

The father of the subject of these memoirs was Captain James Dalton, of the 6th Regiment of Foot, who came of an old Yorkshire family which had been long settled in the East Riding prior to removing into Richmondshire. James Dalton was great-grandson of that Lieutenant-Colonel John Dalton of Caley Hall near Otley, who, on the outbreak of the great Civil War, served under his brother-in-law, the Lord Darcy, in the Royalist army, and was dangerously wounded on July 5, 1643, on passing the bridge of Burton-on-Trent* while conducting Queen Henrietta Maria† from Bridlington to Oxford. Colonel Dalton never

---

* Sir Thomas Tyldesley (as he soon after became) forced the bridge of Burton-upon-Trent by a desperate charge of cavalry.

† On February 22, 1642–3, Queen Henrietta Maria landed at Bridlington, was at York, March 30, at Newark, June 27, and met her husband July 13. See Miss Strickland's *Lives of the Queens of England*, vol. iv. pp. 217–227; edit. 1877.

recovered from this wound, and, after twelve months of ill-health, died at York on July 24, 1644, and received honourable burial in York Minster. The following touching entry was inscribed by Sir William Dalton,* the deceased officer's father, on the fly-leaf of a law-book† where he had chronicled the births and deaths of his children and grandchildren :—

"My only sonne John Dalton was wounded at Burton upon Trente the fift of July 1643 and thereof dyed the 24 or 25th of July 1644, who was A valiant man and A duetyfull and lovinge sonne."

In 1627 Colonel Dalton had married Dorothy Darcy, daughter of Conyers Lord Darcy, by Dorothy, daughter of Sir Henry Bellasis, Knight and Baronet, whose wife (Ursula) was daughter of that Sir Thomas Fairfax of Denton who had served as a soldier of fortune in Italy and Germany. Besides other issue, Colonel Dalton left at his decease two sons, William and Thomas. William, the eldest son, was knighted by Charles II. for the services he and his father had

---

* Sir William Dalton, of Hauxwell, Knt., Attorney-General to the Northern Court at York, was knighted at Whitehall, April 28, 1629. He married Theophane Booth, of the ancient family of Booth of Killingholm, Lincolnshire. He died in January 1649, and was buried in York Minster.

† This interesting old book, with its quaint family registers, is in the possession of the Rev. C. B. Norcliffe, Langton Hall.

rendered during the Civil Wars. The second son, Thomas, settled at Bedale, and, marrying Anne, daughter of Sir Marmaduke Wyvill, Bart., of Constable Burton, was father of John Dalton of Bedale, who, dying in 1701, left an only child, James.

On May 2, 1718, in the nineteenth year of his age, James Dalton was gazetted Ensign in the Royal Warwickshire Regiment of Foot, then commanded by Colonel Robert Dormer, being the 6th Line Regiment. In the following month he joined in Dublin. A good idea of the state of Ireland may be gathered from a general order issued to the officers commanding His Majesty's Forces in that kingdom :—

"Whereas His Grace the Lord Archbishop of Dublin, one of the Lords Justices of the Kingdom, is going on his Visitation to Kilkenny, and that it will be for His Grace's safety to have a guard to attend him on some parts of his Road thither and back again, where the country is infested with Tories, Robbers, and Rapparees, these are to direct and require you to send with His Grace the Lord Archbishop such a number of men through such parts of the Road, leading to and from Kilkenny, as His Grace shall think fit to attend him for his safety. Each party when relieved are to return to their former Garrison. The Civil Magistrates being to provide them with convenient quarters on their march according to Law. Given, &c., 28 May, 1718."*

In July 1719 Dormer's regiment marched from Dublin to Limerick, where it was stationed some time. James Dalton was made Lieutenant on August 29, 1721, and a year or two after was appointed subaltern to the Grenadier Company of his regiment. There is a tradition in his family that his sword and pistols were by no means idle during his long service as a subaltern officer in Ireland, and that the duels he fought earned him the *sobriquet* of "Fighting" Jem Dalton. He married Miss Elizabeth Smith of Limerick, and had an only child, John Dalton, the subject of this memoir, who was born about the close of 1725 in Dublin, or Dublin County, where Dormer's regiment was then stationed.

In the summer of 1739 ten regiments on the Irish establishment, of which Guise's, late Dormer's, was one, were brought over to Britain. Stirring times were at hand. Another war between Great Britain and Spain having become inevitable, the army was increased and the establishment of Guise's regiment was augmented. This augmentation promoted James Dalton to be captain, his commission being dated

* From a copy in the Record Office of Ireland, Dublin.

January 19, 1739–40; and John Guise, the colonel of this regiment, was made a brigadier-general.

Early in 1740 six regiments of marines were raised to serve under Admiral Vernon in the West Indies. A war with Spain—a war in itself just and necessary, and entered into by the repeated advice of both Houses of Parliament — was most popular. The enthusiasm through the country was intense. Officers on half-pay, and those civilians who desired commissions, flocked up to London in large numbers to try and get appointed to the new regiments. The newspapers gave out that some considerable enterprise would be undertaken as soon as the marine forces were ready for service. Recruiting went on so merrily that the six marine regiments of about one thousand men each were speedily formed. George II., finding the war so popular, ordered four more marine regiments to be raised in the autumn of 1740. These additional regiments were raised directly after the first embarkation of the troops, in October 1740, who sailed under the convoy of a naval force commanded by Sir Chaloner Ogle—the troops being under the command of the gallant Lord Cathcart.

One of the four new marine regiments was raised in November 1740, and, in December, Colonel William Hanmer, who came of the old Flintshire family of that name, was appointed to be colonel and captain of a company in the said regiment.* In those days every regiment was called by the name of its then colonel, and accordingly, this marine regiment, which was really the 8th Marines, was called "Hanmer's" Marines. Captain James Dalton applied for and obtained a commission for his son, as second lieutenant in Hanmer's Marines, and, on February 6, 1741, John Dalton—then only fifteen—was appointed to Hanmer's regiment. In those days the Gazettes took little or no notice of subaltern officers, and, in looking through volumes of the *London Gazette*, I find but few promotions or appointments chronicled, under the rank of captain. The information I received from the War Office, fortunately provides me with the date of John Dalton's first commission. I conclude that his first commission was purchased, and a good sum paid for it too, as I read in the *London Daily Post* for "February 19, 1742," that the marine officers who went out with Admiral Vernon's expedition had paid such "vast sums of money for their commissions to *a certain Secretary*, that it was expected that there would be a Parliamentary enquiry about it." I suppose this

---

* "Wm. Hanmer, Esq., to be colonel of a new raised regiment of marines."—*London Gazette*, December 1740.

" extortion " was practised upon all the new regiments, whether they went abroad or not.

Having started our young marine subaltern on his military career, I must return for a brief time to his father, who was with his regiment at Inverlochy in Inverness-shire. Guise's regiment had received orders, in July 1741, to hold itself in readiness to embark on active service. " 'Tis said," wrote a Scotch correspondent of the *London Daily Post* under date of August 25, 1741, "that Guise's regiment and some other troops will immediately embark on board some transports from Clyde for Cork, which is reported will be the place of rendezvous of the force designed for America. His Excellency General Clayton* set out yesterday for Inverlochy where that regiment is quartered." Before this review, which was preliminary to the immediate departure of the regiment, took place, Captain James Dalton had set his affairs in order and executed a deed which provided for his wife's maintenance during his absence abroad, and, in case of his death, left her in sole possession of all his worldly goods. This will, which is short and soldierly, begins as follows :—

" Know all men by these presents I Captain James

* Major-General Jasper Clayton, Colonel of the 14th Regiment and Commander-in-Chief in Scotland, 1741.

Dalton of the Honble. Brigadier Guise's Regiment of Foot to have made constituted and appointed and by these presents to make constitute and appoint and in my place depute Elizabeth Dalton my beloved wife my true and lawfull attorney procuratrix for me the said Captain James Dalton and in my name stead and place to receive from Robert Mitchiner Esqre Paymaster to the said Brigadier Guise's Regiment or any other paymaster who may hereafter be appointed Paymaster to the said Regiment the sum of four pounds sterling money to be payd monthly to her out of my subsistence* during all the days of my lifetime . . . and in the event of my death and of her surviving me then and in that case I hereby give convey and bequeath to the said Elizabeth Dalton my wife all goods and sums of money pertaining and belonging to me or that will be justly due me by bills bonds ticketts accounts arrears of my pay or any other manner or way whatsomever the time of my decease hereby ordaining constituting and appointing the said Elizabeth Dalton my wife my sole executrix of this my last Will and Testament. . . . In testimony whereof I the said James Dalton have hereunto sett my hand and seal at Inverness in North

---

* A captain's pay in 1740 was 10s. a day.

Britain this thirteenth day of August in the year of our Lord one thousand seven hundred and forty-one. . . . JAMES DALTON."*

It is noticeable in this will that James Dalton makes no mention whatever of his only son. He left everything to his beloved wife, and he had but little to leave behind him. His son had been fairly started in life and was expected to make his own way independent of his mother. The son did not fall short of his father's expectations.

Early in September 1741, the Scotch correspondent of the *London Evening Post* sent the following bit of news to that paper, relative to Guise's regiment—Guise's "Geese," as they were jocularly termed by military wags:—

"We hear from Glasgow that Guise's Regiment of Foot is marched for Greenock, in order to be embarked on board the transports for Jamaica; that the officers and soldiers were all well and in high spirits, and that, of the whole regiment, not four private men had deserted."

When it is remembered that nothing but misfortunes and reverses had befallen the British troops since they

---

* From a copy of the original will at Somerset House, London. Registered 156 Boycott.

had left England in the previous autumn, the enthusiasm of all the troops now about to be sent to reinforce the British forces in the West Indies is highly to their credit. The expedition against Carthagena in South America had proved an utter failure, and, what was worse, had cost many brave lives. Fever, dysentery, and epidemics peculiar to the Spanish Main, had decimated the troops. Officers and men suffered alike. Lord Cathcart, the Commander-in-Chief of the land forces, had died of dysentery at the Island of St. Christopher at the very outset of the campaign. He was badly replaced by Brigadier-General Wentworth, between whom and Admiral Vernon, the naval Commander-in-Chief, there was not always the cordial co-operation so necessary for success in a combined naval and military expedition. The reports of the losses and sufferings of the British troops before Carthagena, and in the Island of Cuba, where they were stationed for some months, were fully chronicled in the London papers, and from them copied into other journals. So popular was a Spanish war, however, that when volunteers were called for from other regiments, to raise the regiments ordered on active service up to their war strength, whole companies volunteered for the service, and clamoured to go. Tommy Atkins, a hundred and fifty years ago, looked with the same contempt on a

Spaniard as his sons and grandsons did on the French at the commencement of the great Peninsular War, as recorded in the doggerel :—

> Two d——d Frenchmen, one Portugee,
> One jolly Englishman lick all three!

Nor were the officers any less enthusiastic than the men. The 1st Royals was a two-battalion regiment, and only a certain number of companies were ordered on active service. One battalion was at Cork and the other at Edinburgh. The captains of both battalions agreed to draw lots as to which companies should go abroad. In the *Evening Post* is this entry :—

"Cork, October 6, 1741.—The Captains of the Royal Regiment have drawn lots for the companies to go to the West Indies, and the Lieutenants and Ensigns are to draw lots to-morrow."

Those who drew lucky numbers, as they considered, went with the expedition. Poor fellows! Most of them had drawn their death-warrants, as but few lived to return home. Here is an extract from another London paper showing the martial spirit evinced by all ranks :—

"Cork, October 23, 1741.—All the troops are well and in full spirits, and amount to between 3,000 and 4,000 men. Vast numbers of the men whose lot it was to stay at home are greatly troubled. In one case, where two men had cast lots to go, the one who had to stay had but six shillings in the world, and he gave it to his comrade to go in his stead."*

I find from the *Evening Post* that the fleet, having on board the Royals, Blakeney's and Guise's regiments (Guise's being under the command of Lieutenant-Colonel Murray in the absence of its colonel, Brigadier Guise, who had gone out with the troops in the previous autumn as one of the four brigadiers), sailed from Cork, October 24, 1741, with a convoy of fifty ships, bound for the West Indies.

An epidemic having broken out at the British camp in Cuba, the troops were re-embarked and conveyed to Jamaica in November. The change does not seem to have been profitable, and an English officer writing from Jamaica, early in 1742, to a friend in England, said there was no need for the Spaniards to attack them, as they were dying off as fast as their enemy could wish! The same writer mentions a naval expedition, with a few troops on board, being despatched from Jamaica in the spring of 1742 to make a descent upon some Spanish port; but no good fortune attended it. I believe it to have been in one of these futile expeditions that Captain James Dalton lost his life, as

* *London Daily Post*, Nov. 5, 1741.

he was drowned when making a landing in the West Indies in the spring of 1742. In the *Gentleman's Magazine* for 1742 I find the following notice :—

"Died in the West Indies, from March 8 to May 18, Guise's regiment, Captains Hunt, Bell, and Dalton, and eight lieutenants."

Thus, in less than three months, were half the officers in one regiment swept away. Under date of August 27, in this year, the *London Daily Post* has this sad notice :—

"Various letters from Jamaica bring advice that the last land forces that were sent over thither have been so impaired by sickness that there are not half of them capable to bear arms."

All through the winter months the transports came staggering home, under-manned, ill-victualled, and often without their commanders, who had perished from disease in the West Indies.* These transports brought the shattered remnants of a once fine army. No regiments suffered more than the Marine regiments, as is plainly set forth in the *London Evening Post*.

---

* "No less than forty of the commanders of the transports which took out the troops to the West Indies in October, 1740, died there in the space of a few months."—*London Daily Post*, 1741.

"April 13, 1743. — Yesterday Brigadier-General Blakeney's Regiment of Marines—which consists only of 18 men out of 800, who either died or were killed in the West Indies—landed from Jamaica."

Here is another extract regarding Colonel Robinson's Marine regiment, which had been raised in Yorkshire early in 1740, and had formerly consisted of "picked Yorkshiremen":—

"Some marines arrived from Jamaica say that the unhealthiness of the climate is so great, that of Cochran's and Robinson's marine regiments *hardly anything is left but the names.*"

Captain James Dalton's widow waited until the return of her husband's regiment to Great Britain before proceeding to prove his will, and it was not until May 9, 1743, that the before-mentioned will was proved in London by his widow.

There is no doubt that Captain Dalton left his widow very badly provided for. Being of the younger branch of his family, he had no property of his own, the family property being then in the possession of Sir Charles Dalton, Gentleman Usher of the Black Rod, grandson of Colonel Dalton the Cavalier officer. The pension for a captain's widow in those days was only £26 a year, and I doubt if Mrs. Dalton had much money of her own.

I must now return to her son, and say something about his regiment.

In September 1741, Colonel Hanmer died, and the Colonelcy of the regiment remained vacant till March 1743, when it was bestowed on Lieutenant-Colonel John Duncomb of the Foot Guards. *London Gazette*—"March 1743. Lieutenant-Colonel John Duncomb, to be Colonel of Marines, late Hanmer's, and Captain of a Company." Where the regiment was from 1741 to 1743 does not appear, but I am very certain that it was not on active service, as John Dalton was five years a second lieutenant, which stagnation in promotion meant home service.

Before proceeding to the next landmark in Lieutenant Dalton's career, I must say a few words about the Marine regiments of that time, as they were on a different footing to the present corps of Royal Marines, which was not formed until 1755, and with which the ten Marine regiments of 1740 must not be confounded.

It was the "Merry Monarch" who first introduced Marines into the British service. By his orders six companies of "lande souldiers" were raised as a regiment to serve on board the fleet. This regiment, which was numbered the Third, the Admiral's, or

Duke of York's Maritime Regiment, afterwards became a land corps exclusively, and was eventually honoured by being incorporated with General Monk's proud Coldstream Guards. William III. improved on Charles II.'s "Maritime Regiment," and by his direction two Marine regiments were raised and placed on the establishment of the Royal Navy. Grose, in his *Military Antiquities*, records that, when required, the rank and file were discharged from their regiments and entered on a ship's books, as foremast men, as soon as they became qualified for such duties. Several Marine regiments were levied by Queen Anne to serve with the Fleet and on land, when occasion required, but to serve as soldiers, and not as sailors as in the previous reign. The 30th, 31st, and 32nd regiments of the Line were originally Marine regiments, and the two latter were raised in 1702 to go with Sir George Rooke's fleet to the Spanish coast. After the Peace of Utrecht, in 1713, all the Marine regiments were disbanded, and it was not till the close of 1739, when active preparations were being made for war with Spain, that these popular regiments of "Jollies," as the sailors termed them, were again raised. We have already seen, ten Marine regiments were raised in 1740, and, as they were to go on active service, members of the best families in England were glad to obtain commissions in them. They were purchase regiments and were officered from the Line. Promotion was rapid, and exchanges to and from Line regiments could be easily effected; but all this ceased when the Corps of Royal Marines was raised in 1755. History does not record whether these old Marine regiments were credited with the inordinate amount of tale-believing credulityt hat sailors are said to lay to the charge of the Marines of this century; but as they were a good deal on land in those good old days, they probably had to swallow some strange yarns from "Jack" when they went afloat. Before leaving the subject of the old Marine regiments, it is necessary to state that they ranked after the 43rd regiment of the Line. Thus the 44th was Churchill's 1st Marines, which consisted of ten companies of 100 men each; the 45th was Frazer's 2nd Marines; the 46th was Holmes's 3rd Marines; the 47th was Byng's 4th Marines; the 48th was Cochran's 5th Marines; the 49th was Robinson's 6th Marines; the 50th was Cornwall's 7th Marines; the 51st was Duncomb's 8th Marines; the 52nd was Powlett's 9th Marines; and the 53rd was Sir Andrew Agnew's 10th Marines. In 1747 there were sixty-six Line regiments, including the above ten Marine regiments. When the ten Marine regiments were reduced in 1748 and 1749, the

Line regiments below the ten Marine regiments ranked after the 43rd regiment according to seniority, but none of the regiments were called by their seniority numbers till 1751; before that date each regiment was called after its colonel for the time being.

CHAPTER II.

The Cruise of H.M.S. "Preston," 1743–1748.

On December 12, 1743, John Dalton was appointed 2nd Lieutenant of Marines to H.M.S. "Preston," of 50 guns—then at Spithead—commanded by Captain the Earl of Northesk,* with a complement of 300 men. The Marines only numbered twenty-four, including the officer.

After a short cruise in the Downs the "Preston" returned to Spithead, and in March, 1744, sailed from Portsmouth with Commodore Barnet's squadron for India, and the following extract from the *London Gazette* gives us the object of the expedition :—

"In consequence of applications made by the East India Company to the Lords of the Admiralty, Commodore Barnet, with the ships under his command,

---

* The Right Hon. George Carnegie, sixth Earl of Northesk, was appointed to the "Preston" on September 14, 1742.—*London Daily Post.*

viz., the 'Deptford' and 'Medway' of 60 guns, the 'Preston' of 50, and one of 20, sailed from Portsmouth for India to protect settlements in those parts."

From the muster books of the "Preston" at the Public Record Office, I have been able to trace all the movements of this ship, which, supplemented by extracts from historical works, fill in the history of the "Preston's" cruise and furnish us with mile-stones and finger-posts, speaking metaphorically, in Lieutenant Dalton's early career.

Dec. 12, 1743	. .	Spithead.
Feb. 20, 1744	. .	The Downs.
March 30, 1744	. .	Spithead.
May 2, 1744	. .	At sea.
May 29, 1744	. .	St. Jago.
June 5, 1744	. .	At sea.
August 29, 1744	. .	do.

Extract from the *London Gazette*, August 1744:—

"Letters from Commodore Barnet who arrived at Porto Praya on the island of St. Jago, 26th of May last, with a squadron of His Majesty's ships under his command, gives an account that he found rideing in the road a Spanish privateer called the 'Amiable Maria' of 14 carriage and 12 swivel guns and 79 men, together with a Pink of about 250 Tons under Spanish colours, which he at first took no notice of, having no intention to violate the neutrality of the King of Portugal's Port, but being afterwards informed that Privateer had taken Pink together with a Brigantine and burnt two other English ships which were all at anchor in the Island of May, and whose men they left on that island, the Commodore acquainted the Governor that finding Privateer had so notoriously violated Neutrality of Island of May, he did not think himself obliged to observe any with regard to her, and he accordingly summoned Privateer and Pink to surrender, which they did, and he took possession of them."

Sept. 4, 1744 . .	St. Augustine Bay.
Sept. 13, 1744 . .	Madagascar.
Sept. 21, 1744 . .	At sea.
Nov. 7, 1744 . .	At Prince's Island.
Nov. 14, 1744 . .	Batavia.
Dec. 13, 1744 . .	Anchored off Luceparas.
Feb. 4, 1745 . .	Straights of Sunda.
Feb. 22, 1745 . .	Batavia Road.
April 29, 1745 . .	Sunda.
May 6, 1745 . .	At sea.
June 3, 1745 . .	Off Ceylon.
July 22, 1745 . .	Fort St. David.

The following extracts from Orme's *History of India*, explain the above cruise of the "Preston":—

"War was now declared between Great Britain and France, in consequence of which a squadron of English men of war appeared in the Indian seas. It consisted of two 60-gun ships, one of 50 and a frigate of 20 guns: these ships did not come immediately to the English settlements in Indostan, but passing beyond them cruised in two divisions in the straights of Sunda and Malacca. They took in these stations three French ships returning from China to Europe,* and one returning from Manilla to Pondicherry; the cargoes of which produced £180,000 sterling. . . . After rendezvousing at Batavia, the squadron united appeared on the Coast of Coromandel in the month of July 1745, at which time the garrison of Pondicherry consisted of no more than 436 Europeans; its fortifications were not completed, and no French squadron had hitherto appeared in India."

The French Governor of Pondicherry was so alarmed for the safety of that place, that he asked the Nabob of Arcot to insist with the English Company at Madras that Commodore Barnet should confine his operations to

---

* Commodore Barnet took a French 50-gun ship and three prizes. (Campbell's *Naval History*, vol. iv. page 54.)

the sea. The Nabob being won over to this one-sided bargain, ordered the English Governor to inform the Commodore that no hostilities must take place on land, or he—the Nabob of the Carnatic—would make the town of Madras suffer for it. "This threat," says Orme, "made so much impression upon the government of Madras, that they requested and prevailed on Commodore Barnet to confine his operations to the sea. He therefore sent one of the 50-gun ships to cruise in the road of Balasore at the entrance of the river Ganges, where she took two or three French ships returning from different parts of India to the French settlements in Bengal." The ship sent to Balasore was the "Preston," as the following dates show :—

August 14, 1745 . . At sea.
Sept. 4, 1745 . . . In Balasore road.

From the log-book of the "Preston" for 1745 (now at the Public Record Office), I read that on August 22 she captured the French ship "Heureux," and on September 15 she took a French and a Dutch ship. From the short account given in the log book, I gather that there was a sharp action between the "Heureux" and the "Preston" before the former struck her flag, but the "Preston" only lost one boy in the engagement. The capture of these ships—added to those captured in the straits of Sunda—would give a fair share of prize-money to the officers on board, amongst whom was our Lieutenant of Marines. In those good old days, officers got their full share of prize-money, and had not to wait many years for it as they have now-a-days, and sometimes never get it at all.

Now to return to the cruise of the "Preston":—

Sept. 21, 1745 . .	Off the island Negrais.
Nov. 7, 1745 . .	Do. King's Island.
Nov. 30, 1745 . .	At sea.
Jan. 22, 1746 . .	Fort St. George.
Jan. 29, 1746 . .	Off Pondicherrie.
Feb. 27, 1746 . .	Fort St. David.
May 7, 1746 . .	Off Caricale.
June 9, 1746 . .	Negapatam Road.

Extract from Orme's *History of India*, vol. i. page 62:—

"There was now certain intelligence that a French squadron was preparing to come on the coast of Coromandel, when that of the English was deprived of one of its chief advantages by losing Commodore Barnet, who died at Fort St. David in April. His death, happening at a time when the English affairs in India were threatened with danger, was generally regretted as a public loss; and, indeed, he was a man of great abilities in sea affairs."

On June 25th the English squadron, cruising near Negapatam, descried the French squadron, which consisted of nine ships, and was commanded by De La Bourdonnais, an experienced French admiral. Five of them were 50-gun ships, and on board the ships were 3,300 men. The English squadron consisted of five ships and a frigate, with only half the number of men on board them that the French had. Captain Peyton—as the senior officer—commanded. An engagement took place between the two fleets, but at such a distance that but little damage was done. The fight began at four in the afternoon and finished that evening. The English had 14 killed and 46 wounded. One of the French ships was dismasted and much shattered. Notwithstanding this, Captain Peyton, alarmed at the superior strength of the enemy, called a Council of War next morning, and it was resolved not to venture a second engagement till they were better prepared to meet the enemy.

"When a commander-in-chief," says Campbell, "invested with full power to act by his sole authority, calls a Council of War, it creates a strong suspicion that he wants to divide the blame of an unjust action. . . . Peyton disappeared, and sailed the Lord knows whither."

After the English squadron had refitted in the

harbour of Trincomalee, they proceeded northward, and on the 24th July sighted the French squadron.

"The English," says Orme, "perceiving the addition of cannon, with which the enemy had been supplied at Pondicherry, avoided an engagement. The two squadrons were three days in sight of each other, after which, according to M. De La Bourdonnais' account, the English ships, availing themselves of the advantage of sailing better than the French, disappeared."

Such were the facts of the case, and it is useless to make any remarks about the policy of the English commander. Least said soonest mended. Where he took his squadron will be seen below:—

July 21, 1746 . .	Off Fryer's Hood.
Aug. 23, 1746 . .	Pullicat Road.
Aug. 27, 1746 . .	At Sea.
Sept. 8, 1746 . .	Hughley River.

While the English ships were on their way to Bengal, Admiral De La Bourdonnais prepared to lay siege to Madras. The English Company were much alarmed at these preparations, and applied to the Nabob of Arcot to restrain the French from committing hostilities against them by land.

"But," says Orme, "they omitted to employ the most certain means of obtaining his protection by neglecting to accompany their application for his assistance with a present of money. This ill-judged parsimony left the Nabob so lukewarm in their interests, that, although he did not give M. Dupleix (Governor of Pondicherry) a positive permission, he refrained from making any preparations, or even from using menaces to prevent the French from attacking Madras."

Madras was doomed. The French troops landed four leagues to the south of the town on September 3, and the next day advanced within cannon-shot of the place. After a week's siege, the town was delivered up to the French, and the English surrendered themselves prisoners of war. The French admiral agreed to allow the English to ransom the town, and promised to settle the ransom on easy and moderate terms.* While the siege was in progress, the Nabob of Arcot sent a message to Dupleix, reproaching him for attacking Madras, and threatening to send an army there if the siege was not immediately raised. This message arrived the day that Madras capitulated, and Dupleix, in order to pacify the Nabob, sent him word that the town should be given up to him, and he could make his own terms with the English for their ransoming it.

* Orme, vol. i., page 68.

Bourdonnais, who was a man of high honour and integrity, would not agree to this, and proceeded to treat with the English for the ransom of the town. Dupleix claimed the sole right of disposing of Madras as being Governor-General of the French establishments in India, and the Council of Pondicherry backed him up. Disputes ensued between the two rivals, which, in all probability, saved the English Company from total destruction, as, on September 27, three French ships of war arrived, with a large reinforcement of troops, sufficient to have conquered all the English settlements—which was the intention of Bourdonnais, if Dupleix had not thwarted him in all his plans.

History repeats itself. From the most remote ages down to the present time, that demon Discord and that arch-fiend Jealousy have marred the greatest achievements. Sceptres have fallen, kingdoms have been lost, armies have been routed, the strongest fortresses taken, simply and entirely because those set in authority cannot agree amongst themselves, cannot curb their ambition, and cannot set aside for a moment their own individual interests, even though the enemy be thundering at the city gates. Here is a case in point. If Dupleix and Bourdonnais had only gone hand in hand, they might have carried all before them;

but they let the golden moment pass, and their chance was lost. An enemy who never delays came upon them —the northern monsoon. This terrific hurricane, which rages along the coast every autumn, set in with unusual violence the beginning of October, and six of the French ships in the Madras roads were driven out to sea; five were dismasted and one foundered.

"The articles of the treaty of ransom had been adjusted," says Orme, "the day before the storm happened. It was agreed that the French should evacuate the town by the 4th of October; and by one of the articles the artillery and warlike stores remaining in the town were to be equally divided between the French and English."

Dupleix, who had his own dishonourable schemes in view, insisted on the French retaining Madras for three months, and Bourdonnais was obliged to request the English to accept these terms, which they did, and the treaty was signed on October 10. The ransom of the town was fixed at £440,000. Hardly had Bourdonnais sailed away with his shattered fleet, than the Nabob of Arcot made preparations for seizing on Madras, which he saw Dupleix had no intention of delivering up to him. The Nabob's army laid siege to the town, but was speedily routed by a French detachment sent against it, and the French remained undisputed conquerors of the field. This victory gave Dupleix the pretext he wanted; he declared the treaty of ransom to be null and void.

"The English were enjoined," says the historian Orme, "to deliver up the keys of all magazines without exception—all merchandises, plate, provisions, warlike stores and horses were declared the property of the French Company."

After this flagrant breach of faith the French troops prepared to attack Fort St. David, the stronghold of the English. The English applied to the Nabob for assistance, and he—smarting with the memory of defeat—sent a large force to assist them, and they were thus able to repel the attacks of the French. Thus ended the year 1746, and the beginning of 1747 found the French army before Fort St. David.

In 1746 Captain John Amherst (younger brother of Jeffery, first Lord Amherst) succeeded Lord Northesk as captain of H.M.S. "Preston." Lord Northesk had been long enough on board the "Preston" to form the highest opinion of young John Dalton, and, as will be shown hereafter, the kindness and good-will that existed between the commander of the "Preston" and the young subaltern of Marines was continued by their children.

On December 18, 1746, Lieutenant Dalton was

promoted 1st Lieutenant.* In the winter of this year the "Preston's" movements were as follows:—

Dec. 26, 1746 . .	Ingerlee.
March 7, 1747 . .	Fort St. George.
March 31, 1747 . .	Fort St. David.
April 13, 1747 . .	Do.
April 15, 1747 . .	Off Pondicherrie.

"The squadron," says Orme, "had been reinforced in Bengal by the arrival of two ships, one of 60 guns and the other of 40, sent from England with Admiral Griffin."

The fleet arrived off Fort St. David in March, and Griffin landed with the Marines and sailors. The following extract from the *Evening Post* refers to this event:—

"October 1747.—The East India Company have received advice by an express over land, with an account that the French had been twice repulsed in their siege of Fort St. David in February last, and that, as they were preparing for a third attack, Commodore Griffin appeared before the place with men-of-war, and landed 1,000 men, who obliged the French to retreat with loss of cannon and baggage. After which the Commodore, having been joined by two

* War Office Records.

ships of war, had blocked up Pondicherrie, and, as the Nabob with his Indians had done the same by land, it was thought the place, which is the only settlement of importance that the French possess in the East Indies, must soon surrender for want of provisions. The squadron consists of the following ships :—

"60 guns	York, Princess Mary, Exeter, Medway;
"50 guns	Eltham, Harwich, Preston, Winchester;
"40 guns	The Pearle, Medway's Prize, Lively."

The retreat of the French troops before the English force was probably the first occasion on which Lieutenant Dalton served with the land forces in India, and his first experience of Fort St. David.

Now to return to the "Preston" :—

May 7, 1747 . .	Fort St. David.
May 23, 1747 . .	Poudicherrie.
Sept. 23, 1747 . .	Madrass.
Oct. 31, 1747 . .	Franquematta.

Extracts from the *Evening Post*, 1747 :—

"It is said Commodore Griffin has taken 6 French ships in the Road of Pondicherrie, and destroyed several others, and that he has likewise taken the 'St. Louis,' a French man-of-war of 40 guns. Another account says it was not a man-of-war, but a large ship. Six small trading ships are also said to have been taken by him."

"By the Dutch ships arrived from the East Indies we have an account that the 'Oxford,' Captain Stevens, was arrived at Batavia from Fort St. David to take in arrack for the use of the men of war under Commodore Griffin."

In October most of the ships went to Ceylon to escape the monsoon. In February, 1748, they returned to Fort St. David, where they remained till September. The Marines in all probability were on land most of the time doing garrison duty.

On July 26, 1748, Admiral the Hon. E. Boscawen arrived with a large fleet from Europe. He had been sent out to take the command of the whole squadron in the East Indies, *vice* Commodore Griffin* ordered home. In sporting parlance, Boscawen had been sent to "wipe" Griffin's eye.

---

* Commodore Griffin was promoted to the rank of Rear-Admiral.

The "Preston" was one of the ships ordered home, and while Boscawen was preparing for the expedition to Pondicherry, the "Preston" was being dismantled of her guns and stores for the use of the ships bound for Pondicherry. I gather all this from the log-book of that ship. Here is one of the short daily notices in this book :—

"August 6th, 1748.—Weather . . . Wind . . . Landed all our Marines by order of the Admiral. Killed three bullocks which weighed," &c. &c.

Referring to the ship's muster-book, I find that on August 5 the Marines on board the "Preston" mustered 23, and on August 7 and every succeeding day there was only *one* Marine borne on the ship's books. This luckless man was the officer—Lieutenant Dalton. He was ordered to return with Admiral Griffin, but all his men were sent on shore to join the troops about to march against Pondicherry. If the officers of the ship thought their case a hard one in being ordered home instead of being allowed to take part in the siege of Pondicherry, what must the feelings of the Marine officer have been on seeing himself thus deprived of his men and not allowed to accompany them.

He counted them at break of day,
And when the sun set, where were they?

The ship's officers still had their men and their duties

to attend to. They also could amuse themselves by whistling for the wind, and could d——n it when it came for being a foul one, but a marine had not even this privilege. Referring to this ancient log-book, which was kept by the first lieutenant of the "Preston," I read that while the ships were "rideing at anchor" off Fort St. David, the guns of Admiral Boscawen's ships could be heard firing at Ariacopang, which was being besieged by both land and sea forces. This must have been very galling to the officers and men left behind—sportsmen not allowed to join in the *battue*. The log-book being an official journal, of course says nothing about this. Indeed, it gives few details of any kind excepting the state of the weather, and affairs connected with the ship. For instance, after mentioning the hearing of the reports of the guns bombarding Ariacopang, the writer goes on to say that "two bullocks were killed which weighed" so many pounds. I can fancy the officers at dinner eating their salt junk and bullock's liver, listening to the boom of the distant guns—and cursing their bad luck in not being there.

Early in September the "Preston" and other ships left Fort St. David for Trincomalee Bay; but, before going any farther, I must mention a circumstance which, I think, proves that Lieutenant Dalton had for some months previous to Admiral Boscawen's arrival been on garrison duty in Fort St. David, and was known there. This circumstance is, my finding in the East India Records for 1751 a copy of the last Will and Testament of John Hallyburton, who died in 1751, but whose Will bears the date of August 4, 1748, and the first part of which is as follows:—

"I John Hallyburton late of Madrass, but at this present of Fort St. David, being in Health of Body and Mind do in case of my death make this my last Will and Testament, hereby revoking all former Wills by me made.

"Imprimis I give and bequeath the sum of seventy pounds to my Moor servant Allie Rizzabeag, and to my Christian servant Thomas Morse all my Linnen and wearing apparrell of what kind soever.

"To Mr. Joseph Fowke, Capt. John Holland, Capt. Rodolphus de Gingins, Lieutenant John Dalton, Lieut. George Gardner, Mr. Andrew Munro and Mr. William Belsches each ten pounds sterling for mourning." *

---

* From the fact of his Will being given in the East India Records, I presume he held some Government appointment at Fort St. David. A Mr. David Haliburton gave some valuable information about Lord Clive and Indian affairs to Sir J. Malcolm, when the latter was writing Clive's Memoirs.

Who this John Hallyburton was I do not know, but I infer from the above that Lieutenant Dalton was well known at Fort St. David, and was expected there again. I mention this as it may help to explain subsequent actions of Lieutenant Dalton, and show they were premeditated.

On September 15, 1748, the "Preston" arrived in Trincomalee Bay, and on the 23rd of that month the officers and most of the men were discharged by order, as shown by the muster-book of the "Preston," and amongst the names of the officers discharged is that of Lieutenant Dalton.* The last entry in the log-book of the "Preston" explains this circumstance:—

"Discharged per order into the 'Princess Mary 5 petty officers and 65 seamen.

"The Captain, Commission and Warrant officers were to go on board different ships of the Squadron where they have orders to receive them for their passage home. The boatswain was left in command of the 'Preston,' she being reduced to a hulk."

Hard fate! Reduced from a 50-gun ship to a hulk;

---

* Number 78. Entry, December 12, 1743; discharged per order September 23, 1748, in Trincomalee Bay. (Muster-book of H.M.S. "Preston.")

once commanded by a belted Earl and now under the command of a Bo'sun and a Bo'sun's mate. What became of her after that I know not; there was no one to chronicle the state of the wind, the killing of bullocks and their weight, the broaching of casks of beef, the setting the "sailes," and other such events. Admiral Griffin remained in Trincomalee Bay until he sailed for Europe in January. Whether Lieutenant Dalton returned home with the squadron, or not, remains to be seen.

In October, Admiral Boscawen's fleet arrived in the Bay. The siege of Pondicherry had been raised, and the English lost 1,000 men during the siege, while the French lost very few. Dupleix went so far as to say that the only damage done by the guns from the fleet was the killing of a poor old Malabar woman in the streets of Pondicherry.

Before closing this chapter, I must chronicle the death of Colonel John Duncomb of the 8th Marine Regiment, and the appointment of Lord George Beauclerk to be Colonel of the regiment. *London Gazette*, December 1747: "Lord George Beauclerk to be Colonel of a Regiment of Marines in room of Colonel Duncomb, deceased." Lord George Beauclerk was appointed from the Foot Guards, and in March 1748 he was transferred from the 8th

Marines to a Foot regiment, and Colonel Jorden was appointed Colonel of Marines. *London Gazette*, March 1748: "Colonel John Jorden to be Colonel of a Marine Regiment, *vice* Beauclerk, Colonel of Foot."

CHAPTER III.

Retrospective Sketch of the East India Company's Affairs.—Strength of their Army in 1748.—Peace signed between England and France.—Reduction of the ten Marine Regiments.—Lieutenant Dalton placed upon Half-pay.—He is appointed 1st Lieutenant of an Independent Company by Admiral Boscawen.—Interesting Letter from an Artillery Officer at Fort St. David to a Friend at Woolwich.—Lieutenant Dalton joins the East India Company's Service in 1749, and is made Captain of the Grenadier Company.

THE complete failure of the attack on Pondicherry was a heavy blow to the East India Company. Their foothold on the soil of India had never been very secure, and now the very foundation of their power seemed to be tottering.

Since the reign of Queen Elizabeth this Company had been engaged in extensive commerce in India; but their settlements were few and far between, and confined to the coast. These settlements had either been purchased, or ceded to the Company by Native Princes. Though there were at this time—as there are now—three Presidencies, these Presidencies only consisted of a few factories and fortresses in Bombay, Bengal, and Madras; and, to show the little extent of territory in these Presidencies belonging to the Company, Madras was considered the most important of the three.

Many things had combined together to keep the English so backward. For a hundred years the Portuguese had had the monopoly of the East Indian trade, and, from having the exclusive right of passage to India by the Cape of Good Hope, they were able to defy all other nations; but when their fleet came in contact with the English and Dutch fleets, and this exclusive right was lost to them, their power in India came to an end, and they had to give way before the rising stars of Holland and England. In the 17th century the Dutch were at the height of their commercial prosperity, and the most successful traders in the world. They acquired considerable possessions in the Indian Seas, and their commercial enterprise was far ahead of the English, who confined themselves to their factories and small settlements on the coast of Hindostan. The English also kept themselves aloof from all the quarrels of the native princes, which was—with their limited numbers—a safe policy, but not the way to acquire fame and increased territory. When the French established a trading Company in India, they took a very different course, and proved more formidable rivals to the English than either the Portuguese or Dutch. Their settlements on the coast of Coromandel were contiguous to the British, and whether their countries were at peace or war made little difference to the two rival Companies. "The native powers," says Sir John Malcolm, "by engaging in alliance, and inviting to interference in internal politics, the subjects of one European state, leave to the other, who may be in rivalry or hostility with it, no option between certain ruin, and employing means of self-defence and retaliation. This truth was never more completely evinced than in 1744, when war was declared between England and France. On receipt of this intelligence, the forces under the control of the Companies of the two nations on the coast of Coromandel, prepared to prosecute hostilities by land and sea, upon a scale which involved both in a scene of operations more suited to empires than to commercial factories. The results of these operations will appear wonderful to him who only considers the handful of troops which either party could bring into the field; but the improvements which within the last two centuries had taken place in Europe, gave its soldiers an incalculable advantage over those of Asia, before the latter were taught by repeated defeats to make war upon more equal terms with their European opponents. The superiority of a well-constructed machine over manual labour is not more extraordinary, than the advantages which discipline and the improvements in fire-arms and artillery afford to a regular body of troops over an irregular and badly-armed force. . . . . The well-commanded and well-trained battalion moves amidst ten thousand of its rabble opponents like a giant with a thousand hands, which defend or strike, according to the dictates of one mind, and to whom an unconnected force, where every individual acts for himself, can offer neither injury or resistance."

The great difference between Asiatic and European troops will be easily understood fron this graphic description, given by an experienced soldier and historian, and it will account for the eagerness with which the native princes of Hindostan sought the alliance of the English and French in the constant little wars which at that time convulsed the empire.

The English had by far the best fleet in Indian waters, but the French were the strongest on land, not only in point of numbers, but from possessing well-trained troops and competent engineers. The failure of the attack on Pondicherry was attributed to the want of good engineers more than anything else. At that siege the French had the services of M. Paradis, who was a host in himself and a second Vauban. It was generally said at the time that the failure of the attack on Carthagena, in 1741, was mainly due to the want of engineers,* and it was proposed to remedy this evil by organizing a body of military engineers. According to Clode's *Military Forces of the Crown,* the scientific Corps of Engineers acquired its military character so far back as 1683. But, until May 14, 1757, when they were commissioned by George II., the Engineer officers were as much civilians as soldiers, although by an Order in Council of August 22, 1717, the Engineers became part of the military branch of the Ordnance Department. The few engineers who accompanied Admiral Boscawen's expedition were so badly qualified for their duties that a good deal of the work had to be done by the Artillery.†

Until Major Lawrence‡ arrived in India in 1748, to take command of the Company's troops, there had

---

* *London Daily Post,* Feb. 17, 1742

† After Admiral Boscawen's despatches had appeared in the newspapers a notice appeared in the *Daily Advertiser* of March 16, 1749, to the effect that the Artillery had no connection whatever with the Engineers.

‡ Stringer Lawrence, a brevet major in the British army, was born in 1697, and was many years an officer in Clayton's Foot Regiment (now the 14th). He died a major-general in 1775.

been no officers of experience in that service, and but few troops. There was such a difficulty in obtaining good officers that in 1745 six sergeants of the Foot Guards were offered lieutenants' commissions if they would go out to India, which they did.* The recruits sent out from England by the East India Directors were often the lowest scum in London—the offscourings of prisons and workhouses—and not trained soldiers such as the French had. When Major Lawrence arrived at Fort St. David he found but few troops to command. The plan of training the natives as soldiers had only just been adopted, and as yet but few had been enrolled into the service. With the exception of the Marines on board the fleet, no English regiment had been sent out to India to guard the British settlements there. Since the wholesale destruction of regiments in the West Indies by disease, the "Indies" had a bad name, and the regiments were kept sufficiently employed on active service in Europe. When Admiral Boscawen was ordered to the East Indies in 1747 with a large force under his command, twelve companies of soldiers were raised to accompany the expedition. These companies were called "Inde-

---

* From the *Evening Post*, 1745.

pendent Companies," and were often raised in time of war to go on foreign service.

I find the following notice about these companies in the *Evening Post* of May 30, 1747 :—

"The twelve Independent Companies to be raised are to be draughted six out of the regiments on the Irish Establishment, and six out of the regiments in England, and are to have each a captain, three lieutenants, and an ensign, and the officers, we hear, will be appointed out of those regiments lately disbanded."

These companies each contained a hundred men, and sailed with Admiral Boscawen to India. When the Admiral arrived at Fort St. David, Major Lawrence informed him of the great want of officers, and Admiral Boscawen recommended for commissions two volunteers who came out with him from England, and also James Kilpatrick,* a lieutenant of Marines. In the Company's Records for 1748 I find mention made of only three companies of foot of 100 men each, and a train of artillery commanded by Lieutenant Merriman. From the civil nature of these old records it is difficult to find out the real state of military affairs at that time, but

---

* This officer succeeded Captain Dalton as Commandant of Trichinopoly in September 1753. He saw much service under Clive, and died a major in 1757.

from a few letters and various odds and ends of military intelligence interspersed amongst commercial *miscellanea,* I may safely say that in 1748 there were not 500 European soldiers in the "Presidency of Madras." Major Lawrence found no cavalry at all, and it was not till the close of 1749 that, by his advice, a troop of horse was raised, which was thought a most important step. The command of the troop was given to Captain de Gingins, the senior captain at Fort St. David. Truly the Madras "army" of 1748 was a very small one! It is difficult to imagine a smaller army or one more deficiently officered—in numbers. There appears to have been only one Engineer officer in the Madras Presidency—Mr. George Jones. He was succeeded, on June 13, 1748, by Captain Alexander Delavaux, who was appointed Engineer and captain of the train of artillery at Fort St. David. Such was the "effective list" of the East India Company's forces when Admiral Boscawen arrived at Fort St. David with his fleet, on board which were the twelve Independent Companies, a large body of Marines, and one company of Royal Artillery.

Having given a sketch of the Company's affairs, it is necessary now to return to Admiral Griffin, who was under orders for England.

Griffin was in Trincomalee Bay with a few of his ships, and thither came, after the raising of the siege of Pondicherry, part of Admiral Boscawen's fleet, to avoid the monsoon. In November came the news that peace had been signed between England and France in the preceding April, and, in consequence of this peace, a number of regiments were ordered to be reduced, the ten Marine regiments being among the number. Colonel Jorden's Marines were ordered to be reduced November 8, 1748, and all the officers placed upon half-pay. The news of this general reduction must have been a heavy blow for many of the Marine officers in India, who saw their means of livelihood taken away from them, and but very faint hopes of ever getting on the full-pay list again. Many an officer's life has been blasted by this compulsory retirement, which, fortunately, in these days is seldom resorted to in the case of efficient and deserving subaltern officers. Lieutenant Dalton, accordingly, found himself placed on the shelf at the age of twenty-three, with only two shillings and fourpence per day. The pleasure of going home was quite effaced by this unexpected news, and he resolved to apply to Admiral Boscawen—who was General of Marines as well as Admiral of the Blue—and to offer his services to that popular and kind-hearted commander. As being placed on half-pay released him from all duty, he returned to Fort St. David where Admiral Boscawen had established himself, and offered him his services. The following extract from the official records at the War Office shows the result of his application:—

"Placed upon Half Pay upon the reduction of the Regiment, tho' made 1st Lieutenant in Captain John Fletcher, sen.'s, Independent Companies in the East Indies by Admiral Boscawen."

There must have been many Marine officers in India who, like Lieutenant Dalton, were placed on the shelf, *nolens volens*, and it speaks well for Lieutenant Dalton's character and soldier-like qualities, that he was at once appointed to an Independent Company by the Commander of the sea and land forces. Admiral Boscawen had orders to stay in India till further orders, and he remained at Fort St. David with the troops. The name of Edward Boscawen is a well-known one in the Valhalla of naval heroes. Many anecdotes of his coolness and firmness under the most trying circumstances have been handed down to us, and his "sayings" quoted by various writers. These *bons mots*, like many of the "sayings" attributed to the great Napoleon, are doubtless purely apocryphal, but, as they are characteristic of the person to whom they relate, I may be pardoned for repeating a speech often fathered upon Admiral Boscawen.* It is related of him that, when in command of a British vessel, he was on one occasion hurriedly aroused from sleep by the 1st Lieutenant, who reported that two large French men-of-war were bearing down upon their ship, and asked his commander what he was to do? Boscawen at once angrily replied, "Do? why fight 'em! d——n 'em, to be sure!"

An interesting letter from an officer of the Royal Artillery to a friend at Woolwich was published in the *Evening Post*, in 1749, and is interesting from the graphic account given in it of the "deprivations" of a soldier's life at Fort St. David—a place very often to be mentioned in this narrative.

"Extract of a letter from an Artillery officer, dated Fort St. David's, January 7, 1749:—

"We have no Business here but looking after our men, and no pleasure but waiting on the General; for by the Bye this is as d——d a place as ever men were troop'd in; black women instead of white; boiled Rice instead of Bread, and the Punch Houses such

---

* Boscawen's biographer, in the *Dictionary of National Biography*, now in course of publication, says this speech is imaginary, but at this distance of time it is impossible to tell whether it is or not.

cut-throats that a man need have the Indies to pay their bills. I warrant you think that we have Rack Punch for nothing; but it is a confounded mistake; for in ordering some they brought us so much to pay, in saying it came from Goa or Batavia, that we have been forced ever since to content ourselves with a Drink made of Toddy; a Liquor which would not go down with you at Woolwich. However we are all cheerful and I do not think there is a Man amongst us that would wish to leave this or any other place unless the General was with us. You can't conceive what a Man he is, he is a Father to all under his command, and the Artillery, Sailors, and Independent Companies by his means love one another as Brothers. I never heard them dispute which was the best man, but I have often heard them vye with one another which would do most for their Commander, the Landsmen calling him General, the Seamen, Admiral; the poorest creatures can go to him as easily at all hours as the Governour of the Fort can, and he receives and hears all Petitions without their going through a secretary.

"I must tell you a story of him; Benjamin Walcot, a Matross, who behaved remarkably brave at the taking of the Fort Ariocopang received there many wounds, and though all imaginary care was taken of him, yet upon our return hither he died, and the General would honour his corpse by accompanying it to the Grave saying, '*there was no Honour too great for a man who had fought well and died for the service of his Country.*' This was for a poor Matross. Had you seen him on the death of Major Goodyear* your heart would have bled. These are what have come to my knowledge; the Sailors and Independents can speak of some instances of the like nature; in short if Humanity and sweetness of disposition, if Bravery and conduct, the rewarding of merit, the maintaining Discipline, and the severe punishment of vice, be virtues to speak a man, *Boscawen is he.* We all adore him, and the merchants say they love him."

This officer ended his letter by saying he would not say who was to blame for the failure of the attack on Pondicherry, but "neither General or troops animated by his example could do more than they did against such Engineers, such numbers, and such a Fortification."

In one respect there was little or no difference

---

* Captain John Goodyear (with the local rank of Major in India), was killed at the siege of Pondicherry. He was a gallant and experienced Artillery officer.

between the old Marine regiments and the Royal Marines of a later creation. This similarity was in their being cast aside, when their services were no longer required by their country, and utterly forgotten until grim-visaged war had again to be faced. Most of us have heard the well-known anecdote of William IV. (then Duke of Clarence), who, at a dinner party, threw an empty bottle behind his chair, saying, "There goes a Marine," and, on being asked by an indignant Marine officer who happened to be present what he meant by that remark, the Duke readily replied it was "because he was a good fellow who had done his duty and was ready to do it again." When Lieutenant Dalton was suddenly placed on half-pay and cast aside, like an empty bottle, before he had even a chance of distinguishing himself, he stood much in need of some powerful friend; and to Boscawen, who was as kind a hearted man as ever lived, Dalton owed his future success in life. It was Boscawen who appointed him to Fletcher's Independent Company, and it was Boscawen who, two months after making this appointment, recommended John Dalton to the East India Company at Fort St. David, who were, with the Admiral's help, making an addition to their little army. The officers of the Independent Companies knew that when they returned to England they would be all placed upon half-pay,* and Lieutenant Dalton, having a good knowledge of the Company's affairs from frequent sojourns at Fort St. David, and seeing a fair chance of gaining fame and fortune by staying in India, offered his services to the Company. Again it speaks highly for Lieutenant Dalton's character and abilities that he was offered a captain's commission, and the command of the Grenadier Company† newly formed. He must have been recommended for this post both by the Admiral and Major Lawrence, and when he accepted it, it was on the agreement with Admiral Boscawen that he should be allowed to receive his half-pay when he returned to England for good, as a lieutenant of His Majesty's Service, which he was then entitled to. In the half-pay muster books at the Public Record

---

* The twelve Independent Companies were disbanded in 1750 and the officers placed on half-pay.

† The first introduction of grenadiers into the British army is thus noticed by Evelyn, in his *Diary*, in an account of a review of troops at Hounslow by Charles II. on April 29, 1673: "Now were brought into service a new kind of soldiers called *grenadiers*, who were dexterous in flinging hand granados, everyone having a pouch full; they had furred caps with coped crowns like Janizaries, which made them look very fierce, and some had long hoods hanging down behind, as we picture fools. Their clothing being likewise piebald, yellow and red." —Vol. II. (Edit. 1854), p. 119.

Office, I find the name of Lieutenant John Dalton of Jorden's Marines with 2s. 4d. per diem for the years 1749 and 1750; but after that year, viz. after the return of Admiral Boscawen, his name disappeared from this list altogether.

CHAPTER IV.

The Rev. F. Fordyce *versus* Lieutenant Clive and Captain Dalton.

TURNING over the Fort St. David ledger for 1749 (now at the India Office), which contains an *omnium gatherum* of miscellaneous information, I came upon the account of a Court of Inquiry held at Fort St. David to inquire into the alleged assault upon the Rev. Francis Fordyce, military chaplain at Cuddalore, by Lieutenant Robert Clive; Captain Dalton and Lieutenant John Worth being accused by Mr. Fordyce of inciting Lieutenant Clive to commit the assault.

Any unpublished anecdote of Robert Clive is of interest, and as the above incident bears direct evidence to the friendship which already existed between Clive and Dalton, and which was a life-long one, I have no hesitation in making public an affair which brought discredit on no one except the reverend (?) gentleman who was the plaintiff in the case.

It seems that the Rev. F. Fordyce lodged a complaint againt Lieutenant Clive for having assaulted him, and also accused Captain Dalton and Lieutenant John Worth of being Clive's accomplices, and inciting Clive to assault him. Mr. Fordyce's complaint having come to the ears of the Governor, he was summoned to appear before the Governor and Council at Fort St. David, and to give an account of the affair. Knowing very well what would happen if the true facts of the case came to light, he protested against the inquiry being held, and, on being closely questioned by the Council, he returned very rude answers and abruptly left the room. Lieutenant Clive, Captain Dalton, Lieutenant Worth, and other officers were then summoned, and Lieutenant Clive being asked to give an account of the affair handed in a written statement, which I have copied from the Records, and which is as follows :—

"Mr. Clive's report—

"That being at dinner with Messrs. Dalton and Worth on or about 16th Feb. at Bandipollam, they told him Mr. Fordyce had said to a gentleman in public company that he was a scoundrel and a coward, and that he had shook his cane over him in the presence of Mr. Levy Moses. Mr. Clive further says that some time before this he had been informed by

Captain Cope that Mr. Fordyce did in conversation with him, threaten to break every bone in his skin; and he says that these repeated abuses so irritated him that he could not forbear on meeting Mr. Fordyce in Cuddalore to reproach him with his behaviour, which he told him was so injurious he could bear it no longer, and thereupon struck him 2 or 3 times with his cane, which at last Mr. Fordyce returned, and then closed in with him, but they were presently parted by Capt. Lucas who happened to be by. Mr. Clive further observes he is not the only person who has been abused and calumniated by Mr. Fordyce, who had also aspersed the character of Mr. Joseph Fowke by saying he was a dark, designing villain, that he would slit his nose the first time he met him, and that he had knocked him under the table at the Governor's. He further says Mr. Fordyce had told Captain Dalton at Mr. Belsches' that if everybody would discourse the Governor in the manner he had done, it would alter affairs greatly, that he had talked to him till he had made him quake or shake in his shoes, or words to that effect. Mr. Clive also says Mr. Lindsay told him he had heard Mr. Fordyce say that Mr. Bulkeley was a scoundrel and a coward and that he had shook his cane at him, as he had done at Mr. Clive. Mr. Clive further says he threatened to thrash Mr. Bourchier, and that he had declared to several people he had taken away gentlemen's swords before now, and would pull off at any time his canonicals to do himself justice; and lastly, Mr. Clive says Mr. Lennox told him that Mr. Fordyce was generally shunned and detested both at St. Helena and the West Coast on account of his meddling Disposition which rendered him disagreeable and obnoxious to everyone.

"Signed,

"ROBERT CLIVE.

"Mr. Dalton's report—

"Captain Dalton being asked what he has to say in answer to Mr. Fordyce's allegations against him, his Protest replies:—'That Mr. Rait came to dine with him at Bandipollam the day the affair happened, and told him he had heard Mr. Fordyce say he had called Mr. Clive a Scoundrel and Rascal, and had shook a cane over him, which report he esteeming very injurious to the character of an officer, he thought he could do no less, as a friendship existed between Mr. Clive and him, than acquaint him of it, in order to give him an opportunity to vindicate his reputation, that accordingly he had told Mr. Clive, having first let Mr. Rait know the use he intended to make of his information.' Captain Dalton further says, that Mr.

Worth and he going that evening to Cuddalore in a Chaise saw Mr. Fordyce and Mr. Clive cudgelling each other in the street, whereupon they both jumped out in order to part them, but that it was done before they came up by Mr. Lucas who was in company with Mr. Fordyce at the time, and this is all he knows of the matter.

"Signed,

"JOHN DALTON.

"Before Capt. Dalton withdrew, it being asked him if he had ever heard Mr. Fordyce mention he had spoke to the Governour in the manner so related by Mr. Clive, he replied he had and would give it on his oath; whereupon being sworn he spoke as follows:—'That being one day at Mr. Belsches', though he does not particularly recollect what day, he heard Mr. Fordyce say that if everybody would talk to Mr. Floyer in the manner he had done it would alter the face of affairs greatly, for he had done it till he had made him quake or shake in his shoes or something to that effect.'

"Signed,

"JOHN DALTON.

"Sworn before me in Fort St. David this 3d day of March 1749.

"Signed,

"CHAS. FLOYER."

Lieutenant John Worth gave similar evidence. Captain Cope also had heard Mr. Fordyce speak most abusively of the Company's officers and of their conduct at Pondicherry. A letter from Captain Lucas was then read which testified that Messrs. Dalton and Worth were in no ways concerned in the assault. After which Governor Floyer informed the Council of the insolent conduct of Mr. Fordyce when dining at the Governor's house, and how he had been obliged to reprimand him for the insolent way he spoke of the Company's troops. The Governor also indignantly denied Mr. Fordyce's assertions that he had made him quake or shake in his shoes.

It was unanimously resolved that Mr. Fordyce should be dismissed the Company's service, and a new chaplain was at once appointed to Cuddalore to succeed him.

It has been said by Clive's enemies that he was ever ready to pick a quarrel with anyone, but this is not the case. He never willingly sought quarrels, but was very jealous of his honour and character, which he would suffer no one to speak lightly of. He made very few friends, being naturally reserved and retiring in society; but those he did make he kept through life. John Dalton made friends wherever he went, increasing them like a snowball rolled along snow-covered ground. His frank and open disposition, coupled with the keen sense of humour which distinguished him through life, made him very popular with his brother officers. His friends were chosen with wise discrimination. Lieutenant Worth, with whom he is bracketed above, was a young artillery officer, who had come out to India with Major Goodyear, and had played his part in the unsuccessful attack on Pondicherry. As a young subaltern, hardly out of his teens,* Worth had fought at Fontenoy†—that battle in which the British, unsupported by their Dutch allies, were outnumbered, and had, after repeated gallant charges, to retreat, which so elated the French, that, for many years after, French officers used to encourage their men, when leading them against British troops, by saying, "Come, let us give the English another Fontenoy." It was doubtless from this young Artillerist that Captain Dalton picked up some gunnery instruction, which stood him in good stead later on, when he had to act in the threefold capacity of commander, artillery officer, and acting engineer to the troops placed under his sole command. From Robert Clive—whom Dalton styles in one of his

---

* Appointed a cadet in the Royal Artillery, November 1, 1742. Kane's *Artillery List.*

† Duncan's *History of the Royal Artillery*, vol. i. p. 127.

letters to his mother, "a very intimate and worthy friend of mine"—he could not fail to learn much; for though they were of the same age and neither had so far seen much service, yet was Clive's inborn military genius so great, that his friends and comrades must perforce have seen, even at this early stage of his career, that he was destined to outstrip the most scientific and even the bravest officers in their little army.

CHAPTER V.

The First and Second Expeditions against Devi Cotah.

IN March, 1749, the President and Council at Fort St. David determined to send an expedition against Devi Cotah, a strong fort in the Tanjore country, situated on the coast at the mouth of the Coleroon river.

There were two reasons for undertaking this expedition; the principal one being the desire to obtain possession of a place, so well adapted for commerce, as was reported to the Company by Admiral Boscawen, who had made a reconnaissance of the fort and adjacent country, and strongly advised its acquisition. The other reason was that Sahajee, the deposed king of Tanjore, had come to Fort St. David and craved the assistance of the English, to recover for him the kingdom which his brother Pretaupa Sing had seized. The English had no business to interfere in the matter, but they were very glad of such a good excuse for helping Sahajee, who promised to defray the expense of the expedition, and deliver up the Fort and territory to the English, as soon as they had recovered his rights for him. Accordingly, towards the end of March, the troops under Captain Cope marched for Devi Cotah, with the intention of capturing the Fort, and dethroning Pretaupa Sing the King of Tanjore, notwithstanding his being their old ally and having assisted them against the French.

The force consisted of 430 Europeans with four field pieces and four small mortars. The battering cannon and provisions were sent in four ships.

This expedition, which was badly planned and still worse carried out, was unsuccessful, and the troops had to return, having effected nothing.

Although the President and Council saw that Sahajee's cause was a hopeless one, they were so ashamed of the defeat of their troops, and so anxious for the possession of the fort and territory of Devi Cotah, the value of which had been greatly exaggerated,* that a second expedition was immediately planned, and the command given to Major Lawrence, who had command of all the Company's troops.

---

* Mill's *British India*, vol. ii.

The following despatch* from Major Lawrence to the President and Council at Fort St. David, gives a full account of this expedition, and is noticeable as being the first occasion on which Captain Dalton's name is associated with the Grenadier Company, which company he commanded during his service in India, and, as will be seen by subsequent events, the grenadiers were generally to be found in the hottest parts of the engagements with the enemy.

"An account of the Proceedings of the Forces under the command of Major S. Lawrence from their leaving Fort St. David to the taking of Devi Cotah, and of some transactions after their being in possession of that place.

"May 27th. Embarked the Company's troops at 5 this morning.

"May 29th. Anchored off Devicotah at half-an-hour past 5 P.M. I ordered my own, Capt. Scrimsour's, and Capt. Dalton's Companies with all the Lascars that were in the ships "Exeter" and "Harwich," to disembark in the Roads that Captain Powlett appointed for them, in order to land as soon as the Signal was made with 2 Field Pieces, which were to follow the Boats that landed the Soldiers.

---

* East India Records for 1749.

"May 30th. At 1 P.M. we put off from the Ships in 4 armed Long Boats and several Muscolas. Landed on the Northern shore at 5 o'clock, and drew up about 70 yards from the River, with our front to the Westward, our left flank secured by the river and 1 Field Piece, the right by some bushes and the other Field Piece. We lay upon our arms all night, and sent out small parties of Rangapah's Sepoys which came by land, in front, and on our right flank advanced between one and two hundred yards before the main body, to give timely notice of the approach of the enemy.

"May 31st. The remaining part of our soldiers with some of the Sepoys, landed on the opposite shore at 8 A.M. and then sent their boats to carry over the men I landed before, to join them, which we did about 12 o'clock the same day. I ordered Capt. Dalton with his Company to attack a Redoubt of the enemy's, but finding a deep River between it and him, and it not appearing to be of any great advantage, I ordered him back again, but at the same time sent 2 Field Pieces to dislodge the enemy from thence, that they might not disturb us on the ground we proposed encamping on. We removed some distance from the river side and encamped with our front to the Southward; our flanks secured, the Right by a thick wood and an unpassable

River, the Left by some high sand hills with parties of Sepoys lodged behind them.

"June 2nd. Began to make fascines.

"June 5th. Began to open ground with all our officers and men off duty, and a covering party of 1 Captain, 2 subs., 4 sergeants, 4 corporals, 2 drums, and 60 private men, who were all ordered to observe the greatest silence for fear of drawing the enemy's fire upon them. Upon hearing our men at work, the enemy gave a general discharge round the whole garrison without doing the least execution, the work going slowly on. The covering party and Lascars voluntarily offered to work in the daytime, which I ordered them to do, and had only 3 men wounded.

"June 8th. At daybreak we opened the battery, and gave the enemy three rounds. I then ordered the fire to cease, and beat the Chamade on the battery, at the same time waved a white cloth (which is the custom of the country), to engage them to stop the fire and receive the following summons:—

"'Sahajee Rajah, Lawfull King of Tanjour, having applied to the King of England's Generals and the Honourable East India Company to put him in possession of his kingdom, they have ordered me to lay siege to the Fort of Devi Cotah. As my batteries are now ready to open fire, I send this to let you know that if you will open your gates and receive the troops under my command into the Fort, and acknowledge your lawful Sovereign, your persons and effects shall be safe, and you yourselves well treated; but if on the contrary you obstinately hold out the place, I will beat down your wall, enter your town, and then no man is to expect quarter.

"'Dated in the camp before Devi Cotah, 8th June, 1749.

"'(Signed),

"'S. LAWRENCE.

"'To the Governor of Devi Cotah.'

"I got the letter conveyed by two Bramins at 12 o'clock, but receiving no answer, and the Enemy continuing their fire, I sent orders to our Battery to renew theirs with their Guns and Mortars as warmly as they could, without over-heating the Metal, by which we dismounted most of their Guns, and shattered the wall a good deal with that day's fire.

"June 9th. Received the Governor of Devi Cotah's answer, which was 'that he was upwards of 40 years of age, and had lived hitherto without reproach, and as he had 5,000 men in the place resolutely determined to defend it to the last, he never would sully the small remains of life by surrendering a place he thought impregnable.' The same day we made a considerable breach, but found it repaired by the Enemy next morning.

"June 11th. I applied to Capt. Powlett to land a body of Marines for the security of our Camp while we attacked the place. Accordingly he landed 3 officers and 100 Marines, and we marched at sun-sett from our camp to the Battery and lay upon our arms, expecting to pass the River that Night, but was prevented by a heavy shower of rain which wetted all our ammunition and rendered it impracticable. Mr. Moore the Carpenter of the Train passed the River the same Night, and made fast the rope on the other side to pass our float; as our battery was upon marshy ground I was apprehensive that another day's rain would have made it impossible to attempt anything, I therefore determined to attack the place in the day, which we did on the 12th at 10 o'clock p.m. and performed it in the following order. As soon as we all had passed the river to the number of 700 Sepoys and 400 Military upon the float made by Mr. Moore for that purpose, I first ordered Lieut. Clive with a volunteer platoon of 30 men at the head of 400 Sepoys to drive the enemy from an entrenchment which must flank our left on storming the breach, and 300 more Sepoys on the right to secure our right flank from a large body of Horse, which were posted there for that purpose. Lieutenant Clive accordingly set out for the attack, and met with a deep slough, which we knew nothing of; however, passed it with the major part of his platoon, and attacked the entrenchment, but not being seconded by the Sepoys, and being charged in the rear by the Horse at the same time that he was attacking the entrenchment in front, was obliged to retreat to the slough again, upon which I ordered Sergeant Brown* with the forlorn hope to attack the entrenchment, and, in case of need, Captain Dalton at head of Grenadier Company to support him, but there being no occasion, I immediately ordered Captain Dalton and his Company followed by the main body to attack the breach, which he did, and being joined by Lieutenant Clive and the remainder of his platoon was in full possession by 5 o'clock, and I, at the head of the main body, wheeled one platoon to the right and faced the Horse in order to prevent them from flanking Dalton's Company, and gave them a fire which was so successful that it killed some and put the

* Sergeant Brown was promoted Ensign for his gallant conduct on this occasion.—East India Records, 1749.

rest in such disorder that they went off immediately. We all of us lay that night upon our arms.

"June 20th. I ordered Captain Cope, with his Company and two field pieces and some Sepoys, to take possession of Atchavaram, which he did without any opposition, but on the same night was attacked by the enemy's whole force, and repulsed them with the loss of only 4 men killed and 5 wounded. I marched next morning with another field piece, 120 soldiers, and some Sepoys to throw in provisions, which I did without seeing or meeting with any Disturbance from the enemy.

"The next morning arrived an Ambassador from Camp who made an Apology and said it was a mistake,* and requesting at the same time I would restore them Atchavaram. Upon consideration, finding it would not answer our purpose in opening a communication by land, and that it was much too distant to be relieved from Devi Cotah, and in short that it would not in any way answer our expectation; they at the same time very genteelly offering not to molest or disturb any of our people and to supply us with anything their Camp afforded. After such con-

* There is some obscurity here, most probably some words left out in the copy of Lawrence's despatch.

cessions made on their side, I thought I could with a very good grace deliver them up a place which they with their whole force were not able to take."

The Government at Fort St. David were now able to make their own terms with the King of Tanjore, which they accordingly did, but with very little sense of honour or humanity, as will be seen by the following extract from a learned author :—*

"The reigning King of Tanjore agreed to concede to the English the fort for which they contended with a territory of the annual value of 9,000 Pagodas,† and they renounced support of Sahajee and agreed to secure him and deliver him up to Pretaupa Sing. But for the humanity of Admiral Boscawen this would have been done. He managed to make his escape from the English."

* * * * * *

The close of the year 1749 found the little army of the East India Company remodelled and enlarged. High pay, quick promotion, and the prospect of gaining distinction in the field, as well as other inducements to stay in India, had enabled the East

---

* Mill, vol. ii.

† The Madras pagoda was equal to about three and a half rupees, or about 7s. 8d. in English money.

India Council to procure the services of some of Admiral Boscawen's officers and men. Taken all in all, they might be called a "bobbery pack"; and if they wore any distinctive uniform it was of the "undress" description! For the first time probably in the annals of military history that curious anomaly a "Horse Marine" was to be seen and met with in the precincts of Fort St. David. And he was not a solitary specimen either of this new class of soldier, for there were several Marine officers in the Madras "army" who sometimes marched on foot with the infantry and at other times rode at the head of the dusky mounted followers of the native princes, whose cause the East India Company had espoused for certain reasons which it would, perhaps, be invidious to investigate too closely.

CHAPTER VI.

Rival Princes.—War to the Knife.

IT is recorded of that high and mighty prince Nizam-ul-Mulk, Subadar of the Deccan, that when marching through the Carnatic with an immense army, in 1743, to settle the country, his haughty spirit was sorely troubled at the state of anarchy in which he found this fine province. The great men of the Carnatic—great, at least, in their own estimation—flocked to the still greater Subadar's camp to pay him homage, and had themselves announced to His Mightiness as nabobs. This assumption of authority so enraged Nizam-ul-Mulk, that he turned at last to his officers and exclaimed: "I have seen this day eighteen nabobs in a country where there should be but one; scourge the next fellow who comes with that title!"

Five years after this the great Nizam-ul-Mulk departed for that bourn from which no traveller—not even a Subadar of the Deccan—ever yet returned to tell his experiences. His succession would in these days have been termed a very strong one, as he left six sons behind him; but the sovereignty of the Deccan was claimed by Murzafa-jing, a son of the late Subadar's favourite daughter. This young pretender opposed the somewhat more righteous claims of his uncle—Nazir-jing.* Both claimants flew to arms. As a matter of course, this dispute led to others in the provinces over which the Subadar of the Deccan held sway.

Chunda Saheb laid claim to the nabobship of Arcot, then held by Anwarodean Khan, the true and lawful Nabob of the Carnatic. It was a natural sequence that Murzafa-jing should espouse Chunda Saheb's cause, and that Nazir-jing should support Anwarodean Khan. It also goes without saying that when the French cast in their lot with the two pretenders, the English had no alternative but, sooner or later, to take the opposite side to the French.

The East India Company showed no disposition at first to meddle in this struggle, and for some time

* One of the younger sons.

held aloof, but when the Carnatic was invaded by the combined forces of Murzafa-jing and Chunda Saheb (who were joined by some French troops under the command of M. d'Auteuil), it soon became evident that British interests and British territory would be much endangered if the side which the French had espoused proved victorious. This dreaded contingency came to pass.

A fiercé engagement took place at Amur, fifty miles west of Arcot, and on Anwarodean Khan being shot through the heart, his troops fled, and a large amount of stores and booty fell into the hands of the victorious army. Murzafa-jing and Chunda Saheb proceeded to Arcot, where the latter was proclaimed Nabob of the Carnatic.

The English were alarmed at the success of the French, and Major Lawrence with his troops were recalled from Devi Cotah, after concluding a very satisfactory treaty with the King of Tanjore, who was opposed to Chunda Saheb.

Mahommed Ali, son of Anwarodean Khan, had fled to Trichinopoly, the strongest fort in his dominions. He wrote to the English from thence, asking them for assistance against his rival, and assured them that Chunda Saheb had no right to the title he had assumed, and was a rebel, as well as Murzafa-jing, the real Subadar of the Deccan being Nazir-jing who had been appointed by the Great Mogul.

Soon after these striking events, Nazir-jing entered the Carnatic, and summoned Mahommed Ali to join him from Trichinopoly, and at the same time applied to the English for troops. The English, seeing the cause of Nazir-jing supported by many influential people, and hearing he had an army of 300,000 fighting men, of whom more than half were cavalry, were convinced that he was the real Subadar of the Deccan, and ordered the detachment at Trichinopoly to march with Mahommed Ali to join Nazir-jing at Waldore, fifteen miles from Pondicherry. A few days after this, Major Lawrence arrived with some troops at Nazir-jing's camp. He was accompanied by Mr. Westcott, a Member of Council, and Captain Dalton, who were authorised to treat with Nazir-jing in the interests of the East India Company.

The following extract from Lawrence's "Narrative," refers to this visit to Nazir-jing's camp :—

"Muzapherzing and Chunda Saheb marched out of Pondicherry with their army and 2,000 Europeans, commanded by M. d'Auteuil, with a large train of artillery and a numerous body of Sepoys. They took post within a few miles of Nazir-jing, at whose earnest and repeated request, I marched with 600 men accompanied with Mr. Westcott, one of the Council, with a commission to treat with Nazir-jing, in which we were assisted by Captain Dalton."*

Nazir-jing received the deputation with much politeness, and offered the command of his whole army to Major Lawrence, and wished to engage the enemy at once. This prince's desire for the combat was, however, to be realised in a manner he had not foreseen. Some French officers in the false Subadar's army, discontented at not receiving some of the money bestowed on their fortunate countrymen by the King of Tanjore, whom Chunda Saheb had lately reduced to submission, resigned their commissions and left the camp. M. d'Auteuil, afraid to risk a general engagement with affairs in such a disorganized state, marched back to Pondicherry in the night with his battalion. Deserted by their French allies, the two "false prophets" thought discretion the better part of valour. Murzafa-jing surrendered to his uncle and Chunda Saheb retreated with d'Auteuil, leaving his followers to shift for themselves. The camp was attacked by Nazir-jing, and, the troops being quite unprepared for resistance, many were slain.

Nazir-jing's star seemed now to be in the ascendant;

* See *Memoirs of Colonel Lawrence*, by Richard Owen Cambridge, p. 5.

but, as the French proverb says, "Nothing is certain but the unforeseen." His prosperity was too much for his weak mind. He offended many of his supporters, particularly the Nabobs of Cudapore, Canoul, and Savanore, who conspired against him, and were in league with Dupleix,* the political wire-puller of the situation. A refusal to confirm the grant of territory near Madras to the English East India Company, made to them by Mahommed Ali, induced Major Lawrence to return with his troops to Fort St. David. Shortly after this the French entirely routed Mahommed Ali's army, and then proceeded to attack Nazir-jing, who ordered his nephew's head to be cut off, but Nazir-jing was himself killed by the Nabob of Cudapore, and the troops joined Murzafa-jing. This event caused great joy to Dupleix and Chunda Saheb. Mahommed Ali fled to Trichinopoly, and Murzafa-jing was acknowledged as Subadar of the Deccan.

This French turn of Fortune's wheel was very unpalatable to the English, and filled them with consternation. The Subadar of the Deccan was a very great man in India, as more than one third of the

---

* The Marquis Dupleix, the able Governor of the French East India Company, had married a native a woman of considerable talent, and her knowledge of the Indian character and language was of great assistance to her husband.

6

empire of the Great Mogul was under his control. Dupleix was quite aware of the advantages to be gained from the Subadar, and the glory that would reflect on him and his nation, in having brought about this state of things. Great rejoicings took place at Pondicherry. Dupleix held a court, where he received the compliments of the inhabitants. Murzafa-jing soon came to Pondicherry, and received a great ovation. The day after, the three Patan Nabobs arrived, and demanded the reward of their treachery. Their claims were settled, but not with satisfaction to themselves, and they secretly were resolved to revolt. Dupleix was appointed to collect all the revenues from the countries ruled over by the Subadar, and to account to him for the same, and it was ordered that no money should be current in the Carnatic but such as was coined at Pondicherry. Chunda Saheb was declared Nabob of Arcot, and its dependencies, under the authority of Dupleix. The treasures of Nazir-jing were distributed amongst the conquerors, but Dupleix got the lion's share, and the three Nabobs did not get as much as they had expected. This, added to other disappointments, caused them to revolt on the first favourable occasion. The French and Murzafa-jing marched against the forces commanded by the rebel Nabobs, and so eager was Murzafa-jing to punish them, that he outstripped the French troops, and came up with the Nabob of Canoul and his followers, who were in full flight. Finding he could not escape, the Nabob of Canoul turned round and charged his adversary. Murzafa-jing had his sword uplifted to cut him down, but the Nabob threw his javelin at the Subadar, which struck him on his forehead and penetrated to the brain, killing him on the spot. Thus perished the Subadar, and at the same time the three Patan Nabobs, who were cut to pieces with many of their followers.

The tide of fortune had turned once more, and the victorious and powerful French were thrown into great consternation, by the death of their great ally. Salabat-jing, the eldest brother of Nazir-jing, was proclaimed Subadar of the Deccan, Murzafa-jing only having left an infant son. The newly-elected Subadar agreed to confirm all the concessions made by his predecessor, and to give still greater advantages to the French nation.

CHAPTER VII.

(1751.)

The Nabob, applies to the English for Assistance.—Troops sent to Trichinopoly under Captain Cope.—Revolt at Madura.—Capture of that City by Allum Khan.—Captain Cope offers to retake it.—His Troops lay siege to the Place.—Failure of the Attack.—Their Retreat.—Captain De Gingins sent with a large Force to assist Mahommed Ali.—Capture of Verdachelum.—Affair at Volcondah.—Retreat of the Troops.—Remarks on the same.—French Slanders.—Army retreats to Trichinopoly.—Captain Dalton commands Advanced Post at Wootatoor and defeats the Enemy.—Operations of the French.—Clive's Expedition to Arcot.—English besieged at Trichinopoly by French and Chunda Saheb.—Nabob asks Assistance from the Regent of Mysore.—Captain Dalton defeats a Detachment of the Enemy.—Arrival of a Mahratta Force.—Their Bravery and Success.—Disasters at Kistnavaram.—Death of Captain Cope.—Captain Dalton ordered to proceed to Kistnavaram to take the Command.

IF the affairs of the English East India Company looked gloomy at the close of the year 1750, they did not show any signs of improvement at the commencement of the year 1751. The native Princes had seen with surprise the success that attended the French arms, and were equally surprised at the inactivity of the British.

Mahommed Ali wrote from his fortress of Trichinopoly, imploring the English to assist him, and they —fearing his making a treaty with Dupleix—determined to support him. Accordingly, 280 Europeans and 300 sepoys were despatched to Trichinopoly under the command of Captain Cope. The Nabob's affairs were in a very critical state, most of the native chiefs having acknowledged Chunda Saheb as Nabob of the Carnatic, and joined the rebel army at Arcot. Mahommed Ali sent a force of 2,500 horse and 3,000 peons,* with a detachment of 30 Europeans, under the command of one of his brothers, to settle the Government of Tinevelly, a city 160 miles south of Trichinopoly, and capital of a territory. Lieutenant Innis commanded the Europeans, and had great difficulty in keeping the native troops from revolting.

A revolt had broken out at Madura, the capital of a territory of the same name, which lies between Trichinopoly and Tinevelly. The city had been taken by Allum Khan, a soldier of fortune, who had corrupted the garrison, and held the city for Chunda Saheb, whom the troops acknowledged as their sovereign. The loss of the territory of Madura deprived Mahom-

---

* A name for the infantry of the Deccan, who were armed with broadswords and sometimes with matchlocks

med Ali of more than one-half of his dominions, and was a most serious misfortune. Captain Cope offered to retake the capital. He marched from Trichinopoly with one siege- and three field-pieces, and a small body of Europeans, accompanied by 600 of the Nabob's cavalry, commanded by one of the Nabob's brothers. On their march they were joined by the army from Tinevelly. Arrived at Madura, the troops found the outer wall of the city had several large breaches in it, so that the fire from the siege-guns soon demolished a part of the inner wall; but the shot being soon expended, and the breach not accessible from want of fascines, it was necessary to storm the place. The sepoys, having been brought up to the mark by presents and promises of future rewards, went to the attack very spiritedly. The troops passed the first wall, but at the foot of the breach in the second were met by three champions in armour, who defended the pass with their swords, and were with difficulty killed. The troops then mounted the breach and gained the parapet, where the enemy had, on each side of the entrance, flung up a mound of earth, on which they had laid horizontally some palm-trees, through the interstices of which they thrust their pikes. At the bottom of the rampart within the wall they had flung up a strong intrenchment with a ditch, and 3,000 or

4,000 armed men were ready to defend this work. The troops, wounded by the pikes, were obliged to fall back, with a loss of 90 killed and wounded. The following day Captain Cope prepared to return to Trichinopoly. Mahommed Ali's troops took advantage of this repulse to openly revolt, and 500 horse with 1,000 peons went over to Allum Khan, before the English broke up their camp, and a few days after 2,000 horse deserted.*

Mahommed Ali, having heard that Chunda Saheb was preparing to march from Arcot against Trichinopoly, again appealed to the English, and promised them considerable territory near Madras. The English were roused to action by the constant insults they received from the French. Dupleix had, at the commencement of harvest, put the coping-stone to his insolence, by planting white flags in all the fields which belonged to the French; these flags were plainly visible from Fort St. David, and some were even planted in English territory. This insult stung them to the quick, and they determined to make a desperate attempt to retrieve their fallen fortunes.

Major Lawrence had returned to England, in October 1750, for the benefit of his health, and Captain De

* Extracted from Orme, vol. i. pp. 169–70.

Gingins was senior officer at Fort St. David. Early in April he was sent in command of a force of 500 Europeans (the troop of horse being included), 100 Caffres,* 1,000 sepoys, and 8 field-pieces, and was ordered to wait near Fort St. David till joined by the Nabob's troops from Trichinopoly. After waiting six weeks, he was joined by 600 horse and 1,000 peons. He then proceeded westward, and came in sight of Verdachelum, a large and strong pagoda garrisoned by 300 of Chunda Saheb's army. The garrison were summoned by the Nabob's officers to give up the place. On their refusal, the English troops opened fire on them from the cover of a bank, and, in the evening, prepared to make a general assault; but at sight of the scaling-ladders the enemy at once capitulated.

We now come to the operations of the English troops before Volcondah, which ended in the retreat of the English and their allies, and was certainly an unfortunate affair. Captain Dalton gives a full account, in his Journal, of the proceedings of the troops, and, as he was a prominent actor in the forthcoming scenes, I feel justified in giving his version of what two

* Negroes who were brought to India from the Cape, Guinea, or Madagascar.

learned historians* speak of as "the disgraceful affair at Volcondah":—

"After the reduction of this place [Verdachelum], we march'd to Volconda, a fort about 45 miles from Tritchènopoly, and there the Nabob's forces join'd us, under his brother Abdelbobcon (*sic*); there was altogether above 700 horse and 400 sipoys badly arm'd, the rest of his forces having all deserted him and join'd Chunda-saib, since the massacre of the Nizam, who could afford to pay 'em better, having all the revenues of the country in his hands. Here we had intelligence that Chunda was marching towards [us] with an army of no less than 20,000 horse, in conjunction with the French, under Mons. D'auteüil, who were about 700 strong, and near 2,000 sipoys, with 15 pieces of cannon. We had about the same time a reinforcement of 150 men from St. David's, and, as we were resolv'd to wait in this place for the enemy, possessing the fort of Volconda seemed to us a thing of great consequence. The person who commanded it was a relation to the Nabob. However, for the greater security, we desir'd he would admit a detachment, either of ours or the Nabob's people, into it, as we propos'd to encamp under the walls to wait for the

* Colonel Wilks and Sir John Malcolm.

enemy, and put it out of their power to take it. He gave us for answer that the fort was his family estate, which we could not blame him for taking care of, and that he could not admit one party in without giving umbrage to the other. He declar'd he would observe a strict neutrality, and favour neither side, but would pay his revenues to the Nabob as he had always hitherto done, without Chunda prov'd victorious, and by force of arms prov'd himself Nabob of Arcot, in which case self-preservation would oblige him to give it to the conqueror. Could we have believ'd him sincere, the answer was not unreasonable, for 't was manifest enough that, if he favour'd us, and we should chance to be worsted and oblig'd to retreat, he must, of course, have fallen a victim to Chunda's resentment. But, as it did not answer our purpose at that time, we did not think it satisfactory, and desir'd the Nabob would give us leave to attack him while Chunda's army was too far off to give him any assistance. But he would never consent to it, always assuring us his relation was not in any interest but his, till our dragoons intercepted a letter from the Governor to his Vaquil* in the enemy's camp, desiring him to solicit Chunda to march as soon as possible to his

* "A sort of envoy."

assistance, for he had intelligence we intended to attack him. I actually believe, notwithstanding this, that he was no further in Chunda's interest at that time than that, as he thought him the strongest side, policy oblig'd him to incline that way for his own interest.

"The enemy was then arriv'd within 8 miles of us. The fort was between both armies; but we lay nearest it, and had guards placed at the outside of the gates to give us intelligence if any party of the enemy attempted to throw themselves into it. I lay in a tope of trees close under the wall of the fort, with the Grenadier Company, 60 Coffreys, and 100 Sipoys, with 2 field-pieces to support these parties till our main body could come up, which was about a mile farther off. The people of Volconda never made any objection to our being so near and placing these guards, protesting, as they had from the first, that they would observe a strict neutrality and admit neither party within their walls.

"The enemy came often in large bodies of Horse and Sipoys to reconnoitre our camp, but we always prevented 'em by marching out with the advanced guard and repulsing 'em, which put it out of their power to be any sort of judge of our situation. On the other hand they suffer'd us to reconnoitre theirs every day and often ride with no more than 12 troopers within musket shot of their tents. Our army made but a very despicable figure in comparison with that of the enemy, and there was 2 rivers to pass and a steep hill to ascend to get at 'em.

"The Nabob's brother, notwithstanding, was very anxious to attack 'em, but we thought that considering our great superiority of force it would be imprudent to march to 'em under these difficulties. Several consultations were held to study what was best to be done in our present circumstances, and it was at last agreed to bombard the fort of Volconda. It was natural enough to believe the Enemy would march to the relief of the place, and by that means give us an opportunity of having a fair field action with 'em, and if they did not we were sure to reduce the fort, which would be a great point gain'd in the present situation of affairs.

"The citadel of Volconda is built on a high steep rock. It has round towers and some small pieces of cannon mounted on it; the town below joins to it and is surrounded with a pretty good stone wall of about 16 feet high, flank'd with round towers, but has no ditch. In this place the Moors and all the people of distinction reside, and without all is the *petta*, or village, where the poorer sort have their habitations inclos'd with a mud wall and a ditch.

"It was not very probable that the few shells we could throw in a night would make the governor surrender the fort, particularly as Chunda's army lay so very near, who, it was not to be doubted, would take advantage of our having commenc'd hostilities to march to its assistance and gain admittance, after which we could no longer stay where we lay at that time, but must unavoidably be oblig'd to retreat, and our cause consequently suffer. These reasons induc'd some of the officers to propose to Capt. De Gingin, not to throw away bombs which would be visible to the Enemy's army, but in the night to scalade the lower town, where all the principle men liv'd. This we were sure to carry with great ease and without much alarm, and when we were in to let the Governor know, we had no design to meddle with his Citadel, nor would even suffer our people to plunder the town provided he remain'd quiet above and did not interfere in the battle that would shortly ensue.

"'Tis very certain that the lower town once taken he would have very gladly accepted these terms, not to be molested in the Citadel and in all probability we should have gained our point, and oblig'd the Enemy's army to retire. But Capt. Gingin being much indispos'd, unable to [march ?] to the place himself, and of an unfortunately jealous temper which made him mistrust the good will of any who offer'd to give him advice, would not consent to this proposal but persisted in his first scheme of bombardment, and gave me orders, as soon as the first shell was thrown, to attack and burn the village surrounded with the mud wall, in order to increase the confusion. This was done about 8 o'clock at night with only the loss of one man in forcing the barrier, and the whole village which was a very fine one plunder'd and set in flames. Numbers of poor inhabitants lost their lives in this affair, for as they ran out of their houses to avoid being burnt, they were expos'd both to our musketry, and that of their own people from the Citadel and Town walls firing down at us, and this piece of cruelty answer'd no sort of purpose except that possibly it frightened the Governor a little for a while.

"The Citadel after this was bombarded all night and only now and then returned us a stone shot which did us no sort of prejudice. However, as they show'd no sort of inclination to surrender at daylight, we drew off our mortars and join'd our army which was lying on the plain drawn up out of cannonshot of the fort. About 8 o'clock we perceiv'd the outscouts of Chunda's army appear on the top of the hills that were between our Camp and theirs, and soon after their whole army with the French battallion of about 500 men in their front marching pretty fast to gain a deep water course that led directly to the gate of the fort. Nothing was plainer than that it was now our business to possess ourselves of this watercourse before 'em, which we might easily have done as we were much nearer to it than they were. This would have put us between them and the fort. We should have been under cover and they expos'd, and if they offer'd to advance on us over the plain, they must have lost half their people before they could possibly get near us, but we lay still in a state of stupefaction and saw 'em all enter the watercourse, and pushing hard along it to the fort.

"We then stood to our arms and the Commanding Officer ask'd the officers, whether it was their opinion that we could prevent the Enemy from getting in, by advancing upon 'em. I believe this beginning gave none a very extraordinary idea of our success. Notwithstanding which some gave it their opinion that a brisk push might still doe it, as the fire of the fort was very inconsiderable. In consequence of which the officer of the Cofferys showing great readiness was order'd to make what dispatch he could and engage their front, and if possible stop 'em till our main body could come up. I march'd after him as fast as I could, in any order, with the grenadiers, 3 companys of

Sipoys from the right, and a company of Topasses belonging to the Nabob. The Coffreys ran all the way as fast as they could and attacked the French Grenadiers and Sipoys who led their van in so daring a manner, that (assisted by the fire of the artillery from the left of the Battallion, and 3 guns of the Nabob's) they made 'em give way, and abandon their two advanced guns, so precipitately, that they threw the French main body into confusion and they all got for shelter into the bottom of the watercourse firing from thence up in the air, without doing us the least harm. Never was there a finer prospect of a compleat victory, and the French saw it so plainly themselves, that giving over thoughts of relieving the fort, they suffer'd us to stop 'em, and with much adoe got 2 field pieces up on the bank to bear upon our battallion which was marching down in all appearance with a great deal of resolution, to support us, but on receiving about 20 shot which killed a Lieut. and 8 or 9 men the whole went to the right about and march'd towards camp in great disorder without giving us who were advanced the least notice to retire in time.

"The officers say they could not find the Commanding officer to receive orders what they were to doe; and the men declar'd the officers bid 'em retreat. For my part, being considerably advanced from 'em, I am no sort of judge how it happen'd but was never more astonish'd than when I saw 'em going off, and even the Nabob's horse crying out to 'em and upbraiding 'em with their shamefull behaviour.

"Had the French behav'd with spirit and improv'd their advantage, 'twas next to an impossibility that our advanced partys could have got off; but they remain'd in the watercourse and suffer'd us to retreat very leisurely, and carry off the officer who was kill'd and all the wounded. Chunda's vast army too follow'd the example of the French, and kept on the side of the hills a vast way off. Had these made a charge when our battaillon fell into confusion it might have prov'd a fatal day to us; but they were content with the advantage they had gain'd, and when we left the field their whole army came and encamp'd under the walls of the fort, little more than cannon shot from where we lay. I never saw the Nabob's horse so animated as they were that day. They kept close in the rear of our battallion and, tho few, seem'd to despize Chunda's numbers. Abdel Bobcon's horse was shot under him but he immediately mounted another and headed his people. In short we had no excuse for our bad behaviour. It was a scandalous affair, on our side, and the French had nothing to boast of, for they behav'd to the full as ill as we.

"The reader will easily imagine, after what has been related, that on our return to camp, vigorous councils did not prevail amongst us. The commanding officer, who should have exerted himself on the occasion, and endeavour'd to raise the drooping spirits of the people, was sick, and the general opinion of the situation of affairs was manifest on every countenance. The Nabob's people too, either affraid or disgusted at what had happen'd, were packing up their baggage and preparing to leave us. As soon as it grew dark we struck our tents and marched off without any noise for Wootatoor, where we arriv'd about 4 o'clock the next day. There was an 8-inch mortar belonging to the Nabob left by the people on the road which fell into the hands of the Enemy, the carriage it was on having broke down. We lost nothing but a few of our tents, and some hand-grenadoes, which last we buried having no convenience to carry 'em."*

The above graphic account of a very unfortunate affair bears the unmistakeable stamp of truth, and is borne out by the historian Orme, who adds, what Dalton does not mention, that, *when the battalion was seized with a panic, the Captains, De Gingins, Dalton,*

* Dalton's *Journal*, fol. 24-28.

*and Kilpatrick, and Lieutenant Clive, tried to rally them, but in vain.**

Every little circumstance tends to show very clearly that Captain De Gingins was too cautious, and not possessed of enough ability, or self-reliance, to prove a successful leader. The Council at Fort St. David had been astonished by the dilatory action of the man whom they had placed in command over their troops, and fearing that if Volcondah was not taken, the French and their allies would speedily possess themselves of this important fortress, they sent, early in June, a despatch to Captain De Gingins, the contents of which are referred to in the following memorandum given in the East India Company's Records :—

"June — ? 1751. Mr. Robins† volunteers to go to Volcondah, but is not allowed; he and the Board concur that Captain De Gingins be ordered to seek the enemy, and use his utmost endeavour to bring to an engagement, and this as soon as possible, their strength increasing daily by the arrival of their

---

* Orme, vol. i. (edit. 1775), p. 174.

† Mr. Benjamin Robins, successor to Captain Alexander Delavaux, had been appointed on December 8, 1749, Engineer-General and Commander-in-Chief of Artillery in the East Indies. He died, "pen in hand," at Fort St. David, July 29, 1751.—Vibart's *Military History of the Madras Engineers.*

supplies from Europe, and the President is now ordered to write to Captain De Gingins to that purpose."

On the receipt of the President's letter, De Gingins determined to treat the governor of the fort as an enemy, and he bestirred himself somewhat, but in so hesitating and half-hearted a manner, that neither the Europeans nor the native troops under his command felt any confidence in their leader. As commander of the troops, De Gingins was responsible for the unfortunate result of his operations. The historian Orme fully recognised this responsibility; and from personal acquaintance with the officer in question, who was a Swiss by birth, his character of De Gingins deserves to be given :—

"Captain Gingen was undoubtedly a man of courage, and had seen much service in Europe; but having had no experience against an Indian army, fell into the error of imagining that the cavalry of Chunda Saheb would act with all the vigour of which their number and appearance seemed capable."

It is also only fair to add that this was almost the first occasion on which De Gingins held the chief command, and it must be remembered that, though he had seen much service in Europe, it was as a young subaltern, and that in 1747 he was only a second lieutenant* in one of the Independent Companies under the command of Admiral Boscawen.

Captain Dalton having been one of the senior officers at Volcondah, I have searched into the matter, and read the different historical accounts of this action. The two historians who term it a "disgraceful" affair, go into no particulars. They both agree, however, in taking all share of blame from Lieutenant Clive, because he was at that time acting as Commissary to the troops, having resigned his commission in the army, after the siege of Devi Cotah, and returned to his former civil career. As he was present at Volcondah as a non-combatant, holding no military position, he was of course quite exempt from blame. At the same time, anyone who has read Clive's life, will, I think, agree with me in thinking that, when a council of war was held, he would give his advice to the other officers. I should also think that an officer who had distinguished himself at Pondicherry, and had led the assault at Devi Cotah in the most gallant manner, would have been readily listened to on an occasion when so much was at stake. Sir John Malcolm

---

* In the *Army List* for 1754, I find the name of Rodolph de Gingen (on the half-pay list) as second lieutenant of an Independent Company.

naturally enough wishes to show that Clive had no part in the councils which delayed the engaging with the enemy, and helped to frighten the troops. I also wish to show that Captain Dalton was in no way to blame. He was not in command, therefore was not answerable for the cautious policy of his commanding officer. It is necessary to look fully into this affair, because when Clive, some years afterwards—then at the height of fame and fortune—visited Paris, one of the many slanders told of him behind his back by the envious and most low-minded of the Parisians, was that "he had shared in Captain Dalton's panic at Volcondah." This double falsehood came well from a people who had allowed Arcot to be captured by a handful of troops, commanded by only eight officers, six of whom had never been in action before. The writer who mentions this* was himself a foreigner, and quite ready to throw any obloquy on the conqueror of India, and any English officer. His Life of Lord Clive is full of abuse of that great man, not allowing him any virtues whatever, and trying to make out that Clive's victories were more due to good luck than through any military talent. The above false assertion does no harm to Captain Dalton's character, and no one need be ashamed of having been accused along

* Caraccioli, *Life of Lord Clive.*

with Clive—who, like Nelson, knew not fear—of having been seized with a panic. I can quite understand why the French hit upon Captain Dalton as the cause of the panic. Captain De Gingins was a Swiss, which at that time was the next thing to a Frenchman, and accordingly they selected the officer whom they had good reason to hate, he having often defeated them, and baulked all their endeavours to obtain possession of Trichinopoly. Anyone who reads this Life of Clive must feel disgusted at the picture it draws of one of England's greatest heroes, a "heaven-born general" as Pitt called him. I do not condemn the book merely because of the assertion that "Clive shared in Captain Dalton's panic," as I treat that lie with the contempt it merits, but I do condemn the author for raking up a number of stories of Lord Clive's stay in France, whereof coarseness without wit is the characteristic trait.

Now to return to more pleasant matters.

The English, retreating from Volcondah to Trichinopoly, arrived at the valley of Wootatoor, and their proceedings there are thus chronicled by Captain Dalton in his journal:—

"Wootatoor is a strong post for a Camp, between Volconda and Tritchenopoly, about twenty miles distant from either place. There is a Pagoda with a stone wall and some round towers, but no rampart, which makes it easily taken, and has been the reason of its often changing masters during the war. At this time there was a small garrison of the Nabob's people in it. Our army encamp'd close to this place in a sort of valley surrounded by very high rocks, which made their situation very strong, particularly as the road all round is so full of rocks and stones, that no enemy could bring Artillery near it if the least resistance was made. As this is the barrier to the Tritchenopoly country, we determin'd here to wait for the enemy, and I was detach'd with the grenadiers, Coffreys, and a plattoon of the battalion as an advanced guard, to a pagoda (about two miles in the front of the army), overlook'd by a great rocky mountain, on the top of which I placed a strong guard, both as a look-out and to prevent the enemy from taking possession of it. We lay in this situation about a week, without seeing any appearance of the enemy, till one evening a small party of their Horse came down quite close to us, so near that we at first took 'em for deserters, but on seeing 'em draw their swords we made a company of sipoys give 'em a volley, and advancing on 'em with these and the 12 dragoons which I had with me to patrol, we repulsed 'em a considerable distance beyond our advanced guard, and were returning home when Capt. De Gingin hearing some firing came up on horseback with our Capt. of Dragoons, to see what was the matter, and was follow'd by about 150 of the Nabob's horse. These gentlemen rode a little further on, and seeing the same small party of the Enemy's horse hovering at a distance, the Capt. of Dragoons with the 12 troopers and the Nabob's horse, gallop'd after 'em at full speed. I was then very near my post returning with the sipoys, when Capt. Gingin sent for 'em back, I suppose with a view of supporting our horse, upon which I went with 'em to see what would be the event, and Capt. Maskelyne, who had just then met me, did the same. The Enemy's horse flew before ours who continued pursuing 'em till they were fairly led into an ambuscade, where a thousand horse, and full that number of Sipoys with 2 guns, lay conceal'd. We had but just got back to where Capt. Gingin stood, and brought the company of sipoys with us as he desir'd, when we saw our horse returning at full speed with four times their number at their heels in full pursuit of 'em, and their sipoys with above 20 stand of colours coming up as fast as they could run in the rear of 'em. Our horse halted when they join'd us and the Enemy's cavalry to make sure of us, gallop'd in between us and my post, to put it out of our power to retreat. We had not in all above 40 sipoys, with which we forc'd our way full half a mile, and I really believe should have got clear of the Horse alone, notwithstanding their numbers, if the great body of Infantry which came up with us very fast had not dispirited our sipoys. All our hopes was that the officer who commanded the advanced Guard in my absence, would march out to our assistance, but a tope of trees which was between us and him, prevented his seeing what passed. Captain Gingin expressing a great inclination that some one well mounted would endeavour to push through and bring out the Coffery company, I offer'd my service, and Capt. Maskelyne's horse being better than mine, we chang'd, and taking a pistol cock'd in my hand, I watch'd an opportunity when the road was clearest and set out at full speed for the advanced guard. I was closely pursued, but being extreamly well mounted, not more than 4 or 5 could overtake me, and when any of these came near enough to cut at me, presenting my pistol always sav'd me. When I got near my party they gave over pursuing me, and I met the Coffery company coming out, with which I immediately turn'd back to the relief of our sipoys, but unfortunately came too late. Despairing of getting off they had thrown down their arms and were all either cut to pieces or taken prisoners. Captain Maskelyne* was in the number of the latter, but was not hurt. Capt. Gingin and the Capt. of Dragoons,† with the 12 men, were coming away at full speed and pursued by a vast number of the Enemy's horse when we met 'em. But on seeing us the Enemy retreated, and we marched up to the place the action had happen'd, and brought off the kill'd and wounded men, some of the latter miserably cut. Tho our loss in this affair was not very great, it was, notwithstanding, attended with very bad consequences. Our people already dishearten'd by the affair of Volconda, were greatly discourag'd at it, and had conceiv'd a very bad opinion of the management of affairs. Disagreement and caballs among the officers (the usual consequences of bad success) ensued, and never was a more unhappy set of people got together, nor from whom less good could be expected." ‡

The following memorandum in the East India Records for 1751 is an interesting sequel to the above:—

"Fort St. David, July 22, 1751. The President

---

* Edmund Maskelyne, the early friend and future brother-in-law of Clive, served many years in the East India Company's service, but never attained any high rank.

† This was Captain James Kilpatrick, the future commandant of Trichinopoly.

‡ Dalton's *Journal*, fol. 29–31.

acquaints the Board that Lieut. Maskelyne, who came in from Camp a few days ago, gives an account that Captain De Gingins having advice that a Body of the Enemy's Horse was moving towards our army, then encamped at Wootatore, went out attended by Captains Dalton and Kilpatrick and himself, with about 100 Sepoys and a few troopers to reconnoitre, but advancing too far, they were all surrounded by a party of the Enemy's Horse that were lying in Ambuscade. That Captains De Gingins, Dalton and Kilpatrick thereupon mounting their horses made their way thro' them by the assistance of the troopers, and arrived safe in camp, but he (Lieut. Maskelyne) not having a horse was obliged to surrender to the Sepoys, that he was carried prisoner to Chunda Saib who gave him leave to come here on his parole, but not till he had received an answer from Mr. Dupleix to a letter he wrote on this subject. The President further informs the Board that he has advice that a few days after the above accident, the Enemy made a great attack on our advanced guard at Wootatore, which was so bravely defended by Captain Dalton that they were obliged to retreat with a considerable loss without effecting anything. That our troops have nevertheless quitted that Post and retreated across the river very near Trichinopoly, whither the Enemy have followed them, and encamped on the Banks. Captain De Gingins writes that the reasons of his taking this step were the want of provisions, and his apprehensions that the Nabob's people would leave us."

The repulse of the enemy at Wootatoor,* by Captain Dalton, is modestly detailed in his own soldierly narrative, to which I now return :—

"The day after this happen'd [on July 13], the Enemy's army marched from Volconda and encamp'd within 5 miles of my Advanced Post. As it was not to be doubted but I should be attack'd very shortly, I desir'd the Commanding Officer would give me positive orders whether to make my disposition for a vigourous defence of my post or to retire to our main body on the approach of the Enemy. I look'd upon this precaution as necessary in our situation, to put it out of his, or any one's, power to censure my conduct. For since our affairs began to wear an indifferent aspect, every one seem'd inclin'd to throw the blame of any misconduct off himself, to the prejudice of others. As I never could obtain these orders to my satisfaction I asked the opinion of several of the officers on the subject, and as I found 'em all in-

---

* Called Utatoor in Orme's History.

clin'd to think the post should be defended, I took my resolutions accordingly. I was all along of the same opinion myself that the post should be defended and the army march up to support it, for it was very plain that if the Enemy once got possession of it, our army would be too much streighten'd and oblig'd to retreat from Wootatoor, as we had been for the same reason from Volconda. Besides as we had resolv'd to come to a battle with the Enemy, we could never chuse a more advantageous spot than at the Advanc'd Guard, as we should have fought under cover of banks and walls, which form'd natural intrenchments, and the Enemy could not come at us but by marching over a plain expos'd to their shoebuckles, a thing they are by no means fond of. Two days after the Enemy had encamp'd within sight of me, and sufficiently reconnoitred my post. About 6 in the morning their whole body of horse consisting of at least 20,000 men appear'd on the plains all round, and soon after a line of 4,000 Sipoys very regularly drawn up with 7 pieces of cannon in their front and a company of about 100 Portugueze in the service of Chunda Saib, march'd up slowly to the attack, the Cavalry bringing up the rear, excepting a few squadrons which having detach'd themselves from their main body gallop'd in between us and camp. I immediately sent a dragoon well mounted to give the Commanding Officer advice of this, and having made my disposition in the best manner I was capable, had just begun to fire my Artillery on the advanced partys of the Enemy, that were now come within reach, when I received orders to draw my people off, and join the main body which had advanced a little way from Camp to cover my retreat. I confess I was never more embarass'd than on this occasion. Had I been order'd before to retire on the first approach of the Enemy, I might have done it with much ease. But now that we were in a manner ingag'd with such a multitude, who allways exert themselves most when any party retreats before 'em, I really hardly thought the thing practicable, as we had full a mile and a half to march to where our battallion was drawn up to cover us. To conceal my intentions as long as possible from the enemy, I first drew up my main body in good order close behind the Village out of their sight, and then order'd my advanced partys first to send me the 2 guns and then to retreat slowly in good order and form upon my left. The party on the top of the rock was to come down and join at the same time. The officers perform'd every part with great exactness, and we were all join'd and drawn up in good order behind the village, when the Enemy perceiv'd we were going off. They came on at first like a torrent in a very surprizing manner with great shouts, their foot with above 50 stand of colours were on the top of the hill, firing down at us before we got clear of the corner of the village, and their horse came round by the gate of the pagoda at full speed. We retir'd just far enough to be out of the reach of the musketry on the hill and then made a halt. Their Horse by coming round the corner of the village, were close upon us before they expected it, and came swarming round us in front and on both flanks, but as we expected no other, and were ready prepar'd for 'em, we gave 'em such a reception as effectually check'd their first ardor, and was of great service to us afterwards. They wheeled again round the corner of the village to shelter themselves, upon which we gave 'em 3 huzza's and continued our march towards the battallion. They let us after this goe a considerable way unmolested, before they press'd on us any more, but at last return'd horse and foot together and endeavour'd to surround us. Our Coffreys and a few Topasses, with the Plattoon of the Battallion, made a constant fire on 'em, while the grenadiers march'd with recover'd arms as a reserve, frequently facing about and presenting at bodys of the Horse that press'd on us, and recovering their arms when they halted and declined the charge.

In reality our extraordinary retreat that day may be principally ascrib'd to the gallantry and steady behaviour of that company, who have never fail'd to distinguish themselves in every action that happen'd during the war.

"The ground most of the way between our advanced guard and the camp was very favourable to us by being rocky, which made it difficult for the Horse to be so troublesome to us as they otherwise would have been, and we were under no apprehensions from their foot. We were met about half way by 2 plattoons of the Dragoons dismounted under their Captain, who came to our assistance, and covering our left flank were of very great service. In short we arriv'd safe to camp, and form'd in upon the right of the battallion which was drawn up at a little distance from the tents. For when Captain Gingins saw we were out of danger he return'd from where he had been drawn up to cover our retreat. We lost in all but 15 kill'd and wounded, most of which we brought with us." *

The enemy, in the excitement of the chase, had been insensibly drawn on, and now found themselves face to face with the whole British force. Their first thought was to stand their ground and risk a general action,

* Dalton's *Journal*, fol. 32–34.

but a heavy fire from the British artillery made them waver, and a timely advance of the English and their allies shook their resolution. They turned and fled, losing nigh 300 men before they got out of cannon-shot.

Notwithstanding this success, the cautious Captain De Gingins continued his retreat. After a march of eighteen hours, performed without refreshment in the hottest season of this sultry climate,* the troops arrived near Trichinopoly, and took possession of Pitchandah, a fortified pagoda on the banks of the Coleroon, about a mile to the east of Seringham.

Seringham is an island which lies between the Coleroon and Caveri, and contains a strong pagoda. This pagoda, from its position and natural strength, would have answered all the purposes of a strong fortress, and from its being so near to Trichinopoly, would have been a most important place to hold. De Gingins neglected this grand opportunity, although the pagoda had been virtually in his possession—his troops having been admitted within the enclosure by the Brahmins—and continued his march to Trichinopoly, leaving to the French and their ally, Chunda Saheb, a stronghold which they had the good sense to at once occupy—and hold.

---

* See Extract from Dalton's *Journal* in Appendix.

The only post that still held out for the Nabob, outside of Trichinopoly, was Coilady, and that fort was soon captured by a strong detachment sent against it, notwithstanding the gallant efforts made to defend it by Ensign Trusler. This success caused Chunda Saheb to cross the Caveri, and encamp with part of his army to the east of Trichinopoly. In July, a small reinforcement of Europeans and Sepoys were sent from Fort St. David to Trichinopoly, under the command of Mr. Pigot,* a Member of Council, and Lieutenant Clive, who volunteered to accompany the detachment. Soon after this, another detachment was sent to reinforce the Trichinopoly troops. A captain's Commission was given to Mr. Clive, and he was given the command of the reinforcement which proceeded to Devi Cotah, where they were joined by a few more Europeans under the command of Captain Clarke, who took the command of the whole, and they arrived at Trichinopoly after a skirmish with a French detachment, which was entirely routed.

"Notwithstanding," says Orme, "these reinforcements, the English battalion at Trichinopoly did not exceed 600 men, whereas the French had 900, and the

* Afterwards Sir George Pigot, Bart., Governor of Fort St. George, Madras. He was created a baron in 1766, and died in illegal confinement in India, 1777.

troops of Chunda Saheb outnumbered the Nabob's ten to one. The strength of the city,* indeed, rendered the reduction of it very difficult; but the Nabob's army, at the same time that they were incapable of retrieving his affairs, exhausted his treasures, and his revenues were daily cut off by the enemy taking possession of the countries which furnished them."

Captain Clive, having returned to Fort St. David, made the President aware of this state of affairs, and suggested that an expedition should be sent against Arcot, the capital of Chunda Saheb's dominions.

This suggestion was adopted, and Clive was, at his own request, nominated to the command. This expedition was the turning-point of the Company's affairs,

---

* The town is thus described by Orme:—"The city of Tritchanopoly lies about 90 miles inland from the coast, and is situated within half a mile of the southern bank of the Caveri, and about a mile and a half south-east from Seringham. It is a parallelogram, of which the east and west sides extend near 2,000 yards, and the north and south about 1,200. It has a double inclosure of walls, each of which are flanked by round towers built at equal distances from one another. The outward wall is 18 feet high and about 5 feet thick, without rampart or parapet. The inward is much stronger, being 30 feet high, with a rampart of stone decreasing by large steps from the ground to the top, where it is 10 feet broad, and has a thin parapet of stone about 7 feet high, in which are loop-holes to fire through. There is an interval between the two walls of 25 feet, and before the outward a ditch 30 feet wide and 12 deep. . . . In the northern part of the city stands a rock 150 feet high, from which the adjacent country is discovered for many miles round."

as Arcot was captured, and the lost prestige of the English was restored. There are few undertakings in military history which show more boldness and skill both in the planning and carrying out of the undertaking. The inborn military genius that Clive displayed on this occasion filled everyone with wonder and admiration, and paved the way to future high posts, which left him at last on the topmost rung of the ladder of fame, to which his abilities and courage had brought him. As the siege and capture of Arcot are not in any way connected with my narrative, I pass it over, and return to the Nabob's army at Trichinopoly.

The army of Chunda Saheb—assisted by the French battalion—was besieging Trichinopoly. The principal operations of the siege were carried on by the French, who had sent to one of their settlements for a train of battering artillery, and had raised a battery a little to the south of the north-east angle of the town, and at a distance of 1,200 yards from the city walls. Their camp was two and a half miles from the east side of the town, and Chunda Saheb's troops were encamped close to them, and their unprotected flank was secured by a redoubt containing two guns. Besides the above-named battery—where the French had mounted three 18-pounders and three mortars—they had likewise mounted two 18-pounders on a high rock,* situated 2,000 yards directly east of the town, and they also raised a battery of two guns on the island of Seringham, from which they fired across the river at the northern gate of the city. The two last-named batteries were at too great a distance to do any harm, and now that it was too late, the troops began to be ashamed of having retreated before an enemy who showed himself so little capable of doing them harm.

"To save," says Orme, "that part of the wall against which the enemy's principal battery fired, a glacis was raised to such a height as left nothing but the parapet exposed, and the Grenadiers, commanded by Captain Dalton, were posted behind this glacis. An entrenchment was flung up between the French rock and the south-east angle of the town, in which the Company of Caffres were posted to protect from surprises the Nabob's cavalry, encamped to the south; and to oppose the enemy's battery in the island, two guns were mounted close to the southern bank of the river. To infilade these, the French mounted two guns on the same side of the river, but were one night driven from this post by Captain Dalton. . . . The enemy's

---

* This rock was ever afterwards known as the "French Rock."—Orme, vol. i. p. 200.

batteries fired, indeed, constantly and smartly every day, and damaged some houses, but made no impression on the defences of the town; they supplied the defenders with a great number of cannon-balls, all of which had the English mark, being the same which the ships had fired against Pondicherry, with as little effect as they were now thrown away against Trichinopoly."*

Mahommed Ali, finding himself in great straits for troops, money, and provisions, applied for help to the *Dalloway* of Mysore (uncle of the King of Mysore and Regent of the kingdom), and promised to agree to the Regent's terms. The Nabob having ratified the treaty with his oath, the *Dalloway* agreed to assist him. Accordingly he sent a party of 70 horsemen from Seringapatam—the capital of Mysore—with 500,000 rupees. The day after their arrival, there was a skirmish with the enemy, which gave the Mysorean officers a good opinion of the Nabob's English allies, and, as Captain Dalton was in command of the detachment on this occasion, I shall copy the account word for word from Orme:—

"A platoon with two or three companies of Sepoys were sent to cut down wood at a grove situated about

* Orme, vol. i. pp. 200, 201.

a mile and a half south-east from the city. The enemy having intelligence of this detachment, sent a large body of cavalry to cut off their retreat; their march being discovered from the rock in the city, the Grenadiers with some Sepoys and one field-piece were sent to support the first party, and the troop of Mysoreans accompanied them. Captain Dalton meeting the wood-carts loaded, ordered them to proceed to the town by a distant road, and forming the two parties into one column, with the field-pieces in front, marched towards the enemy, instead of proceeding directly to the city. He first met the French dragoons, who halted on a small eminence to reconnoitre, and waited there till they received the fire of a platoon, on which they retreated, to bring up the body of Chunda Saheb's cavalry, who remained at some distance in the rear. These came up some time after at full speed, flourishing their swords, and made a halt within point-blank shot, to draw the fire of the English troops before they charged; but Captain Dalton ordered his men to preserve it, and wait with fixed bayonets in close order. The field-piece alone was fired, and the first shot dismounted three Moors, and a few more discharges put the whole body to flight. They left 22 horses killed on the plain, and the Mysoreans took five prisoners, together with their horses, which at their return a few days after, they carried in a kind of triumph to their own country."

Towards the end of November, the army of the King of Mysore began to arrive at Carour, situated 50 miles from Trichinopoly. A Mahratta force, under Morarow,* had also been engaged by the *Dalloway*, and in December 500 Mahrattas arrived at Trichinopoly. A few days after their arrival, they rode out into the plain, and finding a small detached camp near the French rock, rode into it sword in hand, and carried off everything they found .there, notwithstanding the swarms of Chunda Saheb's cavalry who hovered around them.

The Mahrattas showed themselves to be brave and skilful soldiers, and by their spirited example they roused the English and Nabob's troops to take more active steps in attacking the enemy, and to forego something of their cautious policy which had kept

---

* Colonel Lawrence gives the following description of this Indian "soldier of fortune" in his *Narrative*:—"Morarow is a Mahratta, who by supporting the divisions in the country has made himself considerable from a small beginning, he sides with no party but as he finds his advantage in it, and as easily changes sides; he commands about 3,000 very good horse. When he is not employed or paid by any Prince, he scours the country for himself, and raises contributions where he can get most and with least work. His real master is the Nanah Shah Raja, but he obeys his orders just as they are conducive to his own interest."

them back so long. Innis Khan, the commander of the Mahrattas, formed the design of entrapping the French soldiers into an ambuscade. Having communicated his plan to Captain De Gingins, he sent a detachment of Europeans to assist the Mahrattas, and the plan was so well carried out that 60 French dragoons were lured from their camp, and, falling into the ambuscade prepared for them, 50 were cut to pieces. The Mahrattas were so elated by their success, that they tried to induce the English to give battle at once to the enemy; but the English declined to risk it till the Mysorean army arrived, on which the Mahrattas told them they were not the same kind of men whom they had seen fighting so gallantly at Arcot. The Regent of Mysore having arrived with his army near Carour, and hearing that Chunda Saheb was sending a large body of French troops and sepoys to Kistnavaram, he wrote to Mahommed Ali, asking him to send a strong party of English to his assistance, as he was not accustomed to fight against Europeans. Captain Cope proceeded to Kistnavaram with 140 Europeans, 100 sepoys, and 2 field-pieces. He was instructed to dislodge the enemy at any hazard. They had entrenched themselves very strongly, and were greatly superior to the English in numbers; nevertheless, Captain Cope resolved to attack them. The forlorn hope, finding themselves in a perilous position, refused to leave the shelter of a bank which hid them from the enemy, and Lieutenant Felix, who stood on the top of the bank trying to encourage them to proceed, was shot through the heart, and, soon after, Captain Cope, returning with a platoon from the reserve, was mortally wounded, on which disasters the whole party retreated in disorder.

At this critical state of affairs, Captain Dalton was ordered to proceed to Kistnavaram, to take the command.

CHAPTER VIII.

(1752.)

Dalton arrives at Kistnavaram.—Interview with the Regent of Mysore.—Operations against the Enemy.—The Mysorean army arrives at Trichinopoly.—Clive's Successes in the Carnatic.—Discontent of the Mysoreans and Mahrattas. — Lawrence arrives from England, and marches with a Reinforcement to Trichinopoly.—French try to intercept him.—Skirmishes with the Enemy.—Is joined by Dalton with a large Detachment.—Encounters with the Enemy.—Clive and Dalton gain an Advantage.—Dalton sent with a Detachment to attack Chunda Saheb's Camp in the Night.—Is misled.—Captures Elmiserum.—Takes a Gun from the Enemy on the other side of the Cavery.—Defeats D'Auteuil at Wootatoor and captures Post.—Clive given Command of a large Force.—Dalton joins Clive and serves under him as a Volunteer.—Is wounded at the Reduction of Pitchandah by the Bursting of a Gun.—Result of Clive's Operations against the Enemy.—Fate of Chunda Saheb.—Dalton receives Surrender of the French at Jumbakisna.—Is left Commandant of Trichinopoly by Lawrence.

WHEN Captain Dalton arrived at Kistnavaram, he found the English detachment joined by the van of the Mysorean army, and two days after, the Regent arrived with the remainder of his troops. The whole force numbered 20,000 men. "The Regent," says Orme, quoting from Dalton's *Journal*, "immediately desired a conference with Captain Dalton, whom he received with great politeness, admiring, not without astonishment, the martial appearance and regularity of the English troops; and forming naturally the same high opinion of the French, he declared he should neither expose his men nor lose time in attacking them, but proceed at midnight with half the army directly to Trichinopoly by another road, at some distance on the plain, leaving the rest with Captain Dalton, whom he requested to divert the enemy's attention by a false attack, until he was out of the reach of danger; and, not content with these precautions, he desired that some Europeans might accompany him as a safeguard to his person. These dispositions answering the purpose for which the detachment was sent, Captain Dalton encouraged him in his resolution, and at midnight began to skirmish against the enemy's posts, which he kept alarmed until morning, by which time the rear of the Regent's division was out of sight. This service proved to be much more necessary than it first appeared to be; for such was the military ignorance of the Mysoreans, that they were discovered in the night passing over the plain with ten thousand lights, as if they had been marching in the procession of an Indian wedding.

"The next day, the rest of their army proceeded, desiring Captain Dalton to remain before the village until they were out of sight, and promised to halt and wait for him, but they were no sooner out of danger than they hurried away to join the Regent. Some hours after, the English detachment decamped, and passing by Kistnavaram without molestation from the garrison, returned to Trichinopoly, where they arrived on the 6th of February, and the French soon after recalled their detachment." *

Such was the Mysorean army! An undisciplined rabble—a pack of rapacious wolves, eager for prey, but afraid to attack their enemy.

The King of Tanjore now declared for the Nabob, and sent 3,000 horse and 2,000 foot to Trichinopoly, under the command of Monack-jee. His example was followed by several other native chiefs, who also sent troops, so that the force of Mahommed Ali became on a sudden superior to that of Chunda Saheb. The Mysore Regent now pressed the English to fight, being anxious to obtain possession of certain places promised him by the Nabob; but Captain De Gingins, knowing well the little reliance to be placed on their allies,

* Orme, vol. i. pp. 207, 208.

refused to risk an engagement till the arrival of an English reinforcement.

While these events were transpiring, Captain Clive had followed up his brilliant success at Arcot, by defeating Raja Saheb at Arni, and two months after, defeated both the French and Raja Saheb at Covrepauk.

"The defeat at Covrepauk," says Orme, "succeeding to their former disgraces, entirely broke their force as well as their spirits; their horse either disbanded, or took service with the governors in the provinces who still acknowledged Chunda Saheb; and the French troops and Sepoys were recalled to Pondicherry, where Mr. Dupleix was so incensed against Raja Saheb, that he would not suffer him for several days to appear in his presence. Thus the English successes in the Carnatic recovered to Mahomedally an extent of country 30 miles in breadth, and 60 in length, the usual revenues of which, including that of the famous pagoda at Tripaty, amounted to 400,000 pagodas.

"Three days after their arrival at Fort St. David, the troops were ready to take the field again under the command of Captain Clive, when, on the 15th of March, Major Lawrence arrived from England, and, two days after, put himself at the head of the detachment. It consisted of 400 Europeans and 1,100

Sepoys, with eight field-pieces, who, escorting a large quantity of military stores, marched through the King of Tanjore's country towards Trichinopoly.

"Here the Mysoreans and Morattoes were so much displeased with the precaution of Captain Gingen, who constantly refused to attack the enemy's posts before he was joined by the expected reinforcement, that the *Dalloway* of Mysore, distressed by the great expenses of his army, had more than once been on the point of returning to his own country; however, him the Nabob appeased by making over the revenues of all the districts which had been recovered since his arrival; but Morarow was so exasperated by this inactivity, which deprived his troops of opportunities to get plunder, and removed the prospect of more important acquisitions, which he expected from this war, that he meditated defection and began to treat with Chunda Saheb." *

When Dupleix heard of the detachment being sent to Trichinopoly, he immediately sent orders to M. Law—the French commander—to intercept Major Lawrence's party. The Major arrived on March 26 at a fort belonging to the King of Tanjore, 20 miles from Trichinopoly, where they left part of their stores.

---

* Vol. i. pp. 213, 214.

Hearing that the enemy had posted a large party with artillery at the fort of Coilady, the Major determined to take another road, but his guides, through some mistake—or treachery—led him to the very place he wished to avoid, and the troops were fired on by six pieces of cannon from across the Cavery. This fire was answered from the rear of the English division, while the main body marched on, inclining to the left, which soon took them out of the reach of the fire, but not before 20 Europeans had been killed. The rear division then joined the main body, and they arrived within 10 miles of Trichinopoly that night. Captain De Gingins sent 100 Europeans and 50 dragoons to join them, and at daybreak Captain Dalton was sent with his company of grenadiers, and another company, along with 400 sepoys and four field-pieces, to join the reinforcement when it came in sight. The French and their allies were drawn up in order of battle, between the fortified posts of Elmiserum and the French Rock, while the rest of the army were in a line extending from the French Rock to Chuckleypollam, by the river side; thus the northern approach to Trichinopoly was completely cut off. The Major, hearing of this disposition made to surround him, marched to the south of Elmiserum, and before he came in sight of the enemy he was joined by the allies, which deterred the enemy from attacking him, and at noon Captain Dalton with his detachment, and some of the Nabob's troops also arrived, whilst Morarow with the Mahrattas kept the enemy in check. The enemy's fire soon put the Mahrattas to flight, and they rejoined the allied army. What followed is best given in the exact words of Orme, who, from the knowledge he derived from the actors themselves in these scenes, was able to give a most minute and consecutive account of all that happened :—

"Captain Clive having reconnoitred the enemy, reported that there was a large choultry,* with some stone buildings, not far from the front of the French battalion, which they, busied in forming their line, had neglected to take possession of. On this advice, he was ordered to proceed with the first division of artillery, supported by the grenadiers, as fast as possible to the choultry, whilst the rest of the column moved up slowly in regular order. The enemy, instead of sending forward a detachment to prevent them, contented themselves with cannonading as their battalion advanced, which had approached within 800 yards of the choultry by the time the English detachment arrived there, and now made a push against their

* A building in India for the shelter of travellers, similar to the Turkish caravanserai.

artillery, which was so well pointed, that it kept them at a distance until the rest of the battalion and Sepoys came up. The Confederate troops, unwilling to expose their horses to a cannonade, halted at a distance; but those of Chunda Saheb, commanded by Allum Khan, the governor of Madura, kept close to the rear of the French. A cannonade ensued, the hottest without doubt, for the time it lasted, that had ever been seen on the plains of Indostan; for the French fired from 22 pieces of cannon, and the English from nine. Such of the English troops as were not employed at the guns, found shelter behind the choultry and the buildings near it, whilst the whole of the enemy's army stood exposed on the open plain, suffering in proportion to this disadvantage. The French battalion in half an hour began to waver, and drew off their guns to a greater distance, upon which the English advanced their artillery, and the men of the battalion who supported them were ordered to sit down with their arms grounded, by which precaution many lives were saved. They still continued to retreat, but Chunda Saheb's cavalry kept things sound for some time, and sustained the cannonade with much more firmness than had ever been observed in the troops of India; they were spirited by the example of their commander Allum Khan, whose head was at length taken off by a cannon ball, as he was encouraging them to advance; on which disaster they gave way and retreated likewise. The Captains Clive and Dalton continuing to advance with the first division of artillery, followed the French, who flung themselves into a great watercourse near the French rock, where they were on the point of being enfiladed by a fire that would have made great havoc amongst them; when Major Lawrence, satisfied with the advantage that had been gained, and unwilling to expose the men to more fatigue under such a burning sun, ordered the pursuit to cease. Seven men of the battalion were struck dead by the heat, and 14 were killed or disabled by the cannonade. The French lost about 40 men, and 300 of Chunda Saheb's troops, with 285 horses and an elephant were found dead on the plain. The success of this day might have been much greater, had the Confederate troops behaved with common activity, instead of which they remained at a distance idle spectators, nor could they be prevailed on to make a single charge, even when the enemy's cavalry retreated."

The above will give the reader a good idea of the bravery of the Native allies, and show that the stress of the Indian warfare lay almost entirely on the Europeans, which must account for the seemingly small operations they were engaged in, as compared with modern warfare, but none the less dangerous and hazardous, as everything depended on the Europeans. None knew this better than Major Lawrence, and when he found that the Nabob's troops and the allies would not at once proceed to attack the enemy, because they judged certain days to be "unlucky," he determined to attack the enemy with his own force. On the 1st of April, Captain Dalton was ordered to march with 400 men at night, and, by taking a large circuit, to come in at the eastern extremity of the enemy's camp, which he was to enter, beat up and set fire to. This plan was frustrated by the troops having to trust to native guides to lead them—not knowing the country themselves—and the guides led them into the very centre of the enemy's posts, two miles from Chunda Saheb's camp. The approach of day rendered it impossible to surprise the enemy, and, as they ran great risk of being surrounded, they returned to Trichinopoly as quickly as they could. The French discovering them in their retreat, perceived the danger they had themselves escaped from, and took the resolution of retreating to the pagodas on the island of Seringham. Chunda Saheb opposed this plan, but M. Law would not change his mind, and when the French troops had retreated to the island, those of Chunda Saheb followed. All the French posts were abandoned except Elmiserum. This important place was captured a day or two after by Captain Dalton, and, as it reflects credit on him, I prefer to give the account of its capture from the words of the historian :—

"The next day, Captain Dalton was sent with the company of grenadiers, some Morattoes and Sepoys, to attack Elmiserum. The party had with them two pieces of cannon and a mortar, the transporting of which through bad roads prevented them from arriving near the place before night, when Captain Dalton with two others advanced to reconnoitre. Discovering no centinels, and finding the gate of the wall which surrounds the foot of the rock open, they concluded that the place was abandoned, and entering, began to ascend the steps which led to the pagoda on the summit; but before they got there, the enemy alarmed by the neighing of the horses, ran to their guns and fired upon the detachment, which they discovered, first by the light of their matches and soon after by the blaze of some huts, to which the Morattoes, as is their custom, had set fire. The smoke of the guns, and the darkness of the night, enabled Captain Dalton and his companions to retreat unperceived; and as soon as he rejoined the detachment, he sent some men to lodge themselves under cover of a bank, before the lower gate, where they were directed to remain until morning, in order to prevent the enemy from making their escape. But this party, desirous of signalizing themselves, imprudently exceeded their orders, and entering the lower gate, ran up the steps, and endeavoured to force the doors of the pagoda above, where they were received with a smart fire, which soon obliged them to retreat with five Europeans and ten Sepoys wounded. A reinforcement was immediately sent to take charge of the bank, and all remained quiet until morning, when the enemy seeing that preparations were being made to bombard them, surrendered. Fifteen Europeans, thirty Sepoys and two pieces of cannon, one of them a fine 18-pounder, were found here; the smaller piece of cannon, with some Sepoys, were left to garrison this post: the rest returned with the other gun to Trichinopoly, which was presented to the Nabob as the first which had been taken during the campaign.* Two days after, the grenadiers, who had always behaved with the spirit peculiar to this class of soldiers, gained another advantage. The great men of the allied army complained that they were much disturbed in their daily ablutious in the Caveri, by a gun

---

* The Nabob presented Capt. Dalton with a horse worth £100 for having captured this gun. See letter from Dalton to Captain Baugh in Chap. XII.

which fired from a choultry lying half-way between the pagoda of Seringham and the river. Captain Dalton was sent to attack this post, who concealed his men behind an old wall on the bank of the river, where they waited till near noon, when the great heat of the sun induced a part of the enemy's guard to return to the camp, and the rest to retire into the choultry to sleep; the grenadiers then rushed across the river, which was fordable, and entered the post with so much rapidity that they took the gun, before the enemy had time to fire it more than once; it was brought away without any opposition, for some field pieces had been sent to the river side to cover their retreat." *

The master mind of Clive hit upon an expedient for gaining some decisive advantages over the enemy, which would help to bring the war to a conclusion—a war already very distasteful to the East India Company. The following extracts from Malcolm's *Life of Clive* show what Clive's plan was, and what was done:—"Major Lawrence perfectly appreciating the character of Clive, consulted him on all occasions. By his advice he divided his small force. . . . While half of his troops remained at Trichinopoly, the other half

* Vol. i. pp. 218, 219.

was placed in a position between Seringham and Pondicherry, in order to intercept that intercourse on which the French depended for their support . . . but Clive was the junior captain of his force, and it was not easy to appoint him to such an important command over the heads of so many officers, some of whom had acquired a just reputation. The difficulty Major Lawrence apprehended on this head was, however, soon put an end to, by the open declaration of the allies, that they would not detach the portion of their troops necessary to form this corps, under any other but him who had defended Arcot."

Clive marched from Trichinopoly on April 6. "He passed," says Malcolm, "the Coleroon before daylight, and occupied a pagoda called Samiaveram, seven miles north of that river, and on the high road betwixt Seringham and Utatore, a post of the French on their line of communication with Pondicherry. His first care was to strengthen this position, and to plant cannon so as to command the road both to the north and south. Dupleix on learning the situation of affairs at Tritchinopoly, had detached a party of seven hundred men under Monsieur D'Auteuil, who had orders to proceed to Seringham and take the command from M. Law, with whose conduct the French governor was much dissatisfied." As Clive's operations at

Samiaveram do not concern my narrative, I pass on to the 9th of May, when Major Lawrence sent Captain Dalton with 150 Europeans, 400 Sepoys, 500 Mahrattas, and four field-pieces, to watch the movements of M. D'Auteuil who still remained at Wootatoor. Captain Dalton, having arrived near Wootatoor, found that the French had taken possession of a village two miles from that place, on which he sent a party of Europeans and Sepoys to dislodge them, which they effectually did. He then formed a stratagem to deceive the French commander, and make him believe that the whole of Clive's force had come to assail him. He divided his force into two bodies, who marched to attack each flank of the enemy's line. "The stratagem," says Malcolm, "succeeded. D'Auteuil not only drew his troops within the walls of the village, but evacuated it next morning and retreated to Volcondah, leaving to Captain Dalton's corps the ammunition and supplies he had brought for the troops at Seringham. M. Law, who observed from the top of this pagoda at Seringham the movement of Captain Dalton's detachment, mistook it for that of Clive, and marched upon Samiaveram; but when he found the whole body of the English stationed there drawn up to receive him, he fell back on his position. The detachment from Trichinopoly had received orders to return, but a sudden swelling of the Coleroon rendered that impracticable. Clive determined to take advantage of the state of the river to take the French post of Pitchandah, on its northern bank, which M. Law could not now succour. Captain Dalton, being informed of his resolution, and not wishing to interfere with his command, immediately placed his corps under Clive's orders, and requested to be employed as a volunteer!"

Although Captain Dalton was senior in rank to Clive, he was quite willing to serve under a man who was recognised by all who knew him as having extraordinary talent, and who was as successful as he was daring. Added to this, a friendship existed between the two officers. Sir John Malcolm, who was as good a soldier as he was a learned historian, makes special mention of this occurrence as reflecting great honour on Clive's character. "A higher testimony," he says, "to acknowledged superiority of character cannot be adduced than this temporary resignation of the claims of senior rank by a gallant and able officer, and that at the very moment when he was flushed with the success of the service on which he had been detached." *

Sir John Malcolm, "whose love passes the love of

---

* Malcolm's *Life of Clive*, vol. i. p. 119.

biographers,"* as Lord Macaulay wittily said of him, is very chary of praise to anyone in his book, excepting Clive, whom he lauds to the skies, so that his high opinion of Captain Dalton, as an officer, is worth a good deal.

"The camp of Chunda Saheb near Seringham," continues Malcolm, "was on the south bank of the Coleroon, opposite to Pitchandah. Clive in order to annoy the enemy and to cover his operations against that place, converted into a six-gun battery a high mound on the north bank of the river, which had been raised to prevent its encroachment on the low land. This mound completely commanded the enemy's camp, and was at the same time protected from the guns at Pitchandah. The disorder created by the opening of this battery was great; men, women, children, elephants, camels, horses and bullocks were instantly seen in disordered flight from this unexpected danger, hastening to the banks of the river, which they were however forced to quit by the guns of Trichinopoly, and at last found shelter by forming an encampment out of reach of the English cannon, and at some distance from the pagoda of Seringham.

"This operation upon the most defenceless part of

---

* Macaulay's *Life of Clive*, p. 3.

the enemy's force, probably produced more effect upon the minds of the allies of the French than any of the more substantial successes of the war . . . the incontrovertible proof which an attack like that of Clive gave of their prince and his allies not being able to protect them, spread alarm through all ranks; and that alarm was soon rendered irremediable by the fall of Pitchandah."

In the operations against Pitchandah, one of the English guns burst, killed three Europeans and wounded Captain Dalton,* who was on crutches for a month after.

It would occupy too much space to give a detailed account of Clive's successful operations, but the following extracts will give the reader all the information that is necessary:—

"The successful result of these operations was," says Malcolm, "the capture and death of Chunda Saheb and the surrender of the French troops. . . . Chunda Saheb's fate was unhappy. When M. Law, reduced to distress in the pagoda of Seringham, told him he could no longer afford him protection, Chunda Saheb listened to a deceitful offer of Monackjee, the general of the Tanjore forces, who, instead of that

* Orme, vol. i. p. 230; Dalton's *Journal*, fol. 75–6.

kindness with which he had sworn to treat him, placed him in confinement, and hastened to inform those with whom he was co-operating (the English, the Nabob Mahomedally, the Mysoreans, and the Mahrattas) of the noble prize he had decoyed into his toils; but Monackjee, instead of that applause and profit he anticipated from his treachery, soon found that, while all resolved he should not retain his prisoner, each party was desirous of having him under their own charge. On seeing that they were on the point of quarrelling with his prince, and amongst each other, for the possession of Chunda Saheb's person, he determined, with a cruelty equal to his perfidy, to put that chief to death. The purpose was no sooner formed than executed; and the head of Chunda Saheb was sent to his rival and enemy, Mahomedally."

Before telling of the "generous" way in which Mahommed Ali treated the head of his enemy, I must retrace my steps a little, and mention the surrender of M. Law at Jumbakisna, on June 3, as Captain Dalton had the honour of commanding the advanced guards that day, and of receiving M. Law's surrender.

"It was agreed," says Orme, "that the pagoda of Jumbakisna should be delivered up, with all the guns, stores, and ammunition. . . . The troops with Captain

Clive were then ordered to rejoin the Major's division, and the next morning before break of day, Captain Dalton marched with 250 chosen men, who halted, beating their drums, at an abandoned outpost, within pistol-shot of the walls of Jumbakisna, whilst the Major remained not far off with the rest of the troops drawn up ready to prevent the effect of any treachery; but none was intended, for Mr. Law soon came out with some of his officers, and conducted the detachment into the pagoda, where they formed with their backs to the gate, opposite to the French troops, who immediately flung down their arms in a heap, and surrendered prisoners.* . . . Thus was this formidable army, whose numbers two months before were nearly equal to the Confederates, reduced without a battle, more effectually than it probably could have been by what is generally esteemed a total defeat in the field."

Now to return to Chunda Saheb's head, which was sent to Mahommed Ali directly after the above occurrence.

"The head," says Orme, "was immediately sent into Trichinopoly to the Nabob, who now for the first

---

* "Captain Dalton took possession of Seringam and the French marched out, being about 600 Europeans and 300 Sepoys."—Lawrence's *Narrative*, p. 29.

time saw the face of his rival. After he had gratified his courtiers with a sight of it, they tied it to the neck of a camel, and in this manner it was carried five times round the walls of the city, attended by a hundred thousand spectators, insulting it with all the obscene and indecent invectives peculiar to the manners of Indostan. It was afterwards carefully packed up in a box, and delivered to an escort, who gave out that they were to carry it to be viewed by the Great Mogul at Delhi; a practice generally observed to heighten the reputation of the successful cause; but there is no reason to believe that it was ever carried out of the Carnatic."

However repulsive this conduct may seem, it must be remembered that the actors in it were ignorant heathens, and the conduct of Mahommed Ali was much more excusable than that of His Most Christian Majesty Charles the Second, who ordered the body of his enemy Cromwell to be disinterred and hung in chains, besides heaping every possible indignity on the corpses of others of his enemies.

* * * * *

Before Major Lawrence left Trichinopoly, he selected Captain Dalton as the officer to be left in command of that most important fortress. This was about the middle of June, as I find by the following notice in the East India Records for 1752:—

"Fort St. George, June 29th, 1752.—Letters from Major Lawrence read. He mentions first his having left Captain Dalton in the command at Trichinopoly."

CHAPTER IX.

Dalton's Position as Commandant.—The Nabob's Secret Promises.—State of Affairs in consequence.—Departure of the Nabob's and Lawrence's Forces.—Plots against the Commandant.—His Life in Danger.—Treachery and Bribery.—Counter-plot.—The Marplot of Trichinopoly.—Precautions against Surprise.—Dalton's Letters to the Governor and Council at Fort St. George.

WE have now arrived at the most important period of Captain Dalton's military career. He was left in command of the principal fortress in the Nabob's dominions, on the possession of which fortress depended the future of the Nabob, and the welfare of the East India Company. As Commandant of Trichinopoly, Captain Dalton was to all intents and purposes the Governor of the city; but the nominal Governor was Kiroodin Khan, the Nabob's brother-in-law, a man of a timorous disposition and very weak mind, who left all the responsibility on Captain Dalton's shoulders. It required the greatest tact on the part of the English Commandant to keep the native element quiet, maintain discipline, and take all necessary precautions for the safety of the city, filled as it was with a numerous rabble in the pay of the Nabob. There were many French prisoners confined there also, and outside the walls treachery and deceit reigned triumphant.

The death of Chunda Saheb and the defeat of the French, had not, as might have been expected, finished the war. The Regent of Mysore declared that the Nabob had solemnly sworn to deliver up Trichinopoly to him, in consideration of his alliance, and, now that Chunda Saheb was dead, and the French defeated, he claimed the fulfilment of the Nabob's promise. This promise had been carefully kept from the English, who were thunderstruck when they heard it. They found themselves in the most awkward predicament, as, on the one hand, the honour of their ally was at stake, and, on the other hand, they saw their own interests in great jeopardy. "The English," says Wilks,* "in discovering for the first time the state of the discussion between Nunjeraj† and Mahommed Ali regarding the possession of Trichinopoly, had the mortification to learn that the splendour of their military achievements was associated with the cause of fraud and dishonour. The treaty, attested with all

* Colonel Mark Wilks' *History of Southern India*, p. 178.

† The Regent of Mysore, also called the *Dalloway*.

the accustomed formalities, precluded a recourse to the usual arts of prevarication, and Mahommed Ali, when pressed by Major Lawrence, plainly avowed that he executed that solemn instrument, and confirmed it with the sanctity of a religious oath, without any intention of observing its engagements.

"The spirit of the negociations which ensued may be described in a few words. Mahommed Ali endeavoured to deceive Nunjeraj with new promises, and this personage, who, in addition to his other follies, had lent to his dear ally a sum now amounting to ten lacs of Pagodas, was completely undeceived, and sought with his inferior powers of simulation to retort the deception of a master in the art. Morari Row, as an impartial umpire, meditated to seize the object of discussion for himself."

"Morari-row," says Orme, quoting from Dalton's *Journal*, "conducted himself with so much seeming impartiality, that he was chosen with equal confidence on both sides to be the mediator between them; and the time being fixed for the conference, he came one evening into the city in great state accompanied by two commissaries deputed by the Regent. They proceeded to the Nabob's palace, where Captain Dalton, as commander of the English garrison, was present." This wily diplomatist pointed out to the Nabob the obligations he was under to the Regent who had so materially assisted him (the Nabob) to defeat his enemies; he then demanded in form the delivery of the city and territory of Trichinopoly, according to the Nabob's own agreement. "The Nabob," says Colonel Wilks, "engaged now to cede the fortress and dependencies of Trichinopoly at the expiration of two months, when he should have acquired another place of safe deposit for his family."* "The Morattoe," continues Orme, "highly commended this resolution; and after some other vague discourse he signified an inclination to speak to him in private, and desired the commissaries to withdraw. As soon as they and most of the audience, excepting Captain Dalton, were retired, changing his countenance from the solemnity of a negotiator to the smile of a courtier, he told the Nabob that he believed him endued with too much sense to mind what he said before those two stupid fellows, meaning the Commissaries; 'You must likewise,' said he, 'think that I have too much discernment to believe you have any intention of fulfilling the promise you have now made. How could you answer to the Great Mogul the giving up of so considerable a part of his dominion to such insignificant people; it would be the highest absurdity to think of it. These you may be assured are my real

* Vol. i.

sentiments whatever my private interest may induce me to say to the contrary in public.' The Nabob was not a little delighted to find him in this disposition, for it was his resentment more than the Regent's that he dreaded, and immediately made him a present of a draught on his treasury for 50,000 rupees, promising much more if he could reconcile matters, and divert the Regent from insisting on the letter of the treaty. This the other assured him he would do, though nothing was farther from his intentions. . . . His views were, first by ingratiating himself with the Nabob, to persuade him to admit a large body of Morattoes into the city, as the best means of deceiving the Regent into a belief that he really intended to give it up according to his promise, and these military umpires would have been instructed to seize on any opportunity that might offer of seducing or overpowering the rest of the garrison, and if this iniquitous scheme succeeded, he intended to keep possession of the city, which he had formerly governed, for himself. . . . . The apprehensions of an immediate rupture obliged the English troops who had proceeded on the 16th of June as far as Utatoor to return on the 18th to Trichinopoly, for the Mysorean had even threatened to attack the Nabob if he offered to march out of the city in order to join his European allies, as he had promised. Their appearance, more than their remonstrances produced an accommodation for the present. The Nabob made over to the Regent the revenues of the island of Seringham, and of several other districts, empowering him to collect them himself; promised again to deliver up Trichinopoly at the end of two months, and in the meantime agreed to receive 700 men, provided they were not Morattoes, into the city. On these conditions the Mysorean agreed to assist him with all his force to reduce the Arcot province. Neither side gave any credit to the other, but both expected advantages by gaining time . . . . and the Regent wished for nothing so much as the departure of the Nabob and the English battalion, that he might carry on his scheme to surprise Trichinopoly, which he knew their presence would render ineffectual. The excuses he made when pressed to march, sufficiently explained his intentions, and to frustrate them 200 Europeans with 1,500 sepoys were placed in garrison in the city, under the command of Captain Dalton, who was instructed to take every precaution against a surprise.

"The battalion, now reduced to 500 men, together with 2,500 sepoys, began their march on the 28th of June, accompanied by the Nabob at the head of 2,000 horse."

In the meantime, Dupleix had been appointed Nabob of the Carnatic by Salabat-jing, which title Dupleix conferred on Rajah Saheb, the son of Chunda Saheb; but he turning out incapable, the title was given to Mortizally, who paid Dupleix £50,000. It is not necessary for me to state here the successes obtained by the gallant Lawrence and his able coadjutor Clive, over the French, after their leaving Trichinopoly; I need only say that the victory over the French at Bahoor,* checked the resolution the Mysoreans had taken of declaring openly for the French.

The critical position of the garrison of Trichinopoly, after the departure of the English troops, is very plainly set forth in the narrative of the gallant Lawrence:—

"Nanderauze, the Maisore general, still remained before Trichinopoly, with Morarow, outwardly our friend, but ready to seize the first opportunity to get possession of the town; they therefore kept Captain Dalton continually on the watch, the more so as it was necessary to seem as if we did not suspect them or know anything of their treaty with the French. Mr. Dupleix did not lose so fair an opportunity of endeavouring to bring the Maisoreans to his interest. He therefore promised Nanderauze not only Trichinopoly, but gave

---

* A village between Fort St. David and Pondicherry.

him hopes that the Kingdom of Tanjore might also be added to it." *

Amongst the volumes of East India Records now at the India Office, there is one labelled, "Extra Occurrences, 1751–1753." This contains copies of the most important letters, written and received by the President and Council of the English Company. It contains numerous letters from Captain Dalton during the year and a half of his command at Trichinopoly; and his letters were considered so important, that the President† gave orders that any letters from Captain Dalton should be opened at once, even if he (the President) were absent when they came. I give copies of some of the most important letters, which have all been woven into history.

"June 29th, 1752. Fort St. George.

"Letter from Captain Dalton at Trichinopoly mentioning the steps he had taken for the security of the place, and that the Mysore and Maratta armies remained encamped under the walls, that all his endeavours to persuade them to join our forces have been ineffectual, nothing less than their whole demand will satisfy them. They have, however, promised, if the

---

* Lawrence's Narrative (in Cambridge's *History of the War in India*, 1750–60), p. 37.

† Mr. Saunders, Governor of Fort St. David.

Nabob will sign with his great Chop* to give them what before promised, they will immediately send 4,000 Horse to join our army; this the necessity of the Nabob's affairs have obliged him to comply with, but at the same time he declared to his friends that he had neither design or right to give away this Fort and Country, which belonged to the Mogul, and is under the protection of the English. By this agreement the King of Mysore is to be at liberty, when he goes away, to send 700 Peons into the Fort, which he (Captain Dalton) has consented to, but absolutely refused signing to any other part of the Contract."

"Another letter from Captain Dalton informing the Board of a conspiracy to arm the French prisoners. As soon as he could discover the names of Jemidars concerned, would disarm Sepoys, seize the Ringleaders, turn Mysore Peons out of Fort, and secure Gopaul Rauze,† the King's brother, who commanded them, till further orders."

The Governor and Council at Fort St. George, in their answer to Captain Dalton's last letter, advised

* Seal on which is engraved the name of the Mogul and the year of the Hegira.

† Erroneously supposed to be brother to the Regent of Mysore. "The nations of India employ the term 'brother of attachment' when in the west we should say 'particular friend,' and this term probably led to the mistake."—Wilks, vol. i.

him "to make friends with Maratta Jemidar, but to be extremely cautious he was not deceived under specious pretences. Must not admit any of the troops (Mysoreans) into fort except those already received by agreement." Before this letter reached Trichinopoly the various plots against the safety of the fortress, and the life of the commandant, had come to a head and burst.

The following extracts from Orme will show the extreme difficulty of Captain Dalton's position, and the network of treachery which surrounded both him and the city. His life at this time was not worth a day's pay, as he was the principal object of all the treasonable plots that the crafty minds of his enemies could think of. It required the hundred eyes of Argus to detect the treachery that lurked around, and it was entirely owing to Captain Dalton's precautions, presence of mind, and quick perception, that Trichinopoly—the safety of which was much more to him than his life—was preserved for the Nabob.

"The English battalion," says Orme, "no sooner quitted Trichinopoly, than the regent set about accomplishing his scheme of surprizing the city, and, by disbursing large sums of money, endeavoured to gain 500 of the Nabob's best Peons, armed with firelocks. The Jemidars, or captains of these troops, received his bribes, and promised to join the 700 Mysoreans in the garrison whenever they should rise. Captain Dalton receiving some hints of the conspiracy, kept ward in the city with as much vigilance as if he had been in an enemy's country, and caused the artillery on the ramparts to be pointed every evening inwards on the quarters of the Mysoreans, and of the suspected Peons.

"These precautions naturally alarmed those who had been treating with the regent, but still none of them made any discovery, whereupon at a general review of arms ordered for this purpose, he directed their flints to be taken out of their firelocks, under pretence of supplying them with some of a better sort. This convincing them that their practices were discovered, the Jemidars came and confessed all that had passed, imploring forgiveness; each brought the sum he had received, and that of the principal man was 16,000 rupees. They protested they had no view in taking the money, but to keep their troops from starving, who had scarcely received any pay from the Nabob for nine months, and as a proof that they had no intention of assisting the Mysorean in his designs, they said that not one of them had removed his wife and family out of the city. Captain Dalton made them few reproaches, but ordered them to march with their troops the next morning to join the Nabob's army at Trivadi. The Regent finding this scheme frustrated, hired two fellows to shoot Captain Dalton as he walked on the ramparts, who, luckily receiving intelligence of their design a few hours before they intended to put it in execution, sent a detachment which took them prisoners in the house where they had concealed themselves with their arms. One was sullen and said little, but the other confessed the whole and declared that three more were engaged in the plot, who had undertaken to watch the gate of the palace and shoot Kiroodin Khan,* the Nabob's brother-in-law, when he should come out on the tumult which the death of the English Commander would naturally occasion; but these, on seeing the soldiers march to the house, had made their escape. The Regent when reproached for this treachery denied that he had any knowledge of it. He employed however Morari-row to sollicit the pardon of the assassins, and the friendship of the Morattoe being at this time thought very valuable, Kiroodin-Khan granted his request, but did not reprieve the men before they had gone through the ceremony of being fastened to the muzzles of two field-pieces in sight of the whole garri-

---

* This name, like most of the Indian names, is spelt differently by every historian. The reader will perceive that the names were generally written according to the pronunciation alone.

son drawn up under arms. Five days after, two other Mysoreans came to another Jemidar who commanded 180 sepoys at one of the gates of the city, and attempted to seduce him; but this officer, an old and faithful servant of the Company, secured the fellows and carried them to Captain Dalton. The articles signed by the regent were found on them, which leaving no room for equivocation, they confessed the act, and were the next morning blown from the muzzles of two field-pieces. This execution struck such a terror that the regent could not get any more of his own people to undertake such commissions, and having remained quiet for some days, he at length pitched upon one Clement Poverio,* a Neapolitan, who commanded a company of Topasses in the Nabob's service, and had often the guard over the French prisoners in the city. This man trading a good deal, went frequently into the camp of the Mysoreans, which gave the regent an opportunity of making application to him in person. He assured Poverio that he had, besides the Mysoreans in garrison, a strong party in the city, and offered great rewards if he would join

---

* This officer subsequently lost a leg in an action near Trichinopoly, and by Major Lawrence's strong recommendation, was granted a pension of fifteen pagodas per month by the East India Company.—*East India Records.*

them on the first commotion. The Neapolitan gave him cause to believe he was to be wrought upon, but said he must first sound the disposition of his officers, and on his return he made a faithful report to Captain Dalton of what had passed. He was ordered to return to the camp the next morning with instructions how to proceed, and conducted himself so dexterously, that a few conferences intirely gained him the confidence of the regent. Having settled the plan of operations, he brought to Captain Dalton the agreement signed by the regent and himself, sealed with the great seal of Mysore; it was specified that Captain Poverio should receive 20,000 rupees for himself, and 3,000 more to buy firelocks, in order to arm the French prisoners, who were to be let out the first time his company took the guard over them; he was at the same time to seize on the western gate of the city, near which the Mysoreans were encamped, and to hoist a red flag, on which signal the whole army were to move and enter the town."*

Captain Dalton's plan to catch the Mysoreans in the trap which they had laid for him, would undoubtedly have been successful, and saved the garrison a good deal of after trouble and bloodshed, had not the

* Orme, vol. i., pp. 257–59; Dalton's *Journal*, fol. 97–102.

Governor—Kiroodin Khan—with his usual timidity, and weakness of mind, stopped the enterprise.

Lawrence's account of the "Marplot" of Trichinopoly is worthy of notice:—

"The Governor of Trichinopoly acquainted Nanderauze of Dalton's design. . . . When he had done this he acquainted Captain Dalton with it, not a little pleased with himself, and thinking he had acted with uncommon discretion in the affair to prevent the Mysoreans' design by such a prudent step. . . . Nanderauze wisely desisted from the attempt, but offered large sums for Poverio, dead or alive. It was on the discovery of this that I proposed Dalton should seize on the Maisorean and Morarow, which he might easily have done by a surprize, as he often had conferences with them; and I must own I thought in justice it would have been right to have done it, but the Presidency were of another opinion."*

Now to return to Captain Dalton.

"Fort St. George, July 27th, 1752.

"Letter from Captain Dalton telling he had not been able to let the Mysore plot come to a head, through the fears of the Nabob.† . . . The King lays the plot on one of his Jemidars, though his own Chop

---

* Lawrence's *Narrative*, pp. 38, 39.

† Meaning Kiroodin Khan.

proves the contrary. . . . The King wished to bribe him (Captain Dalton) by the means of his Debash to deliver up the fort for 2 lacs of rupees and offered Debash 12,000 rupees if he could accomplish it." (A lakh of rupees equals £12,500.)

The following extract from Orme shows what preparations had been made by the Commandant to entrap the Mysoreans, and how the Governor acted the part of Marplot:—

"On the day fixed for the execution of this enterprize, all the cannon that could be brought to bear on the Mysore camp were well manned, and above 700 musketeers, Europeans and Sepoys, were concealed in the traverses and works near the western gateway with a great number of hand grenades; the rest of the garrison was under arms, and the Mysoreans would certainly have suffered severely, but the fears of the Nabob's brother-in-law put a stop to the enterprize. He was apprehensive that the attempt might succeed, and to avoid the risque, sent a messenger to upbraid the regent and to acquaint him that the garrison was prepared to receive him."

"The mutual distrust," continues Orme, "increased daily, although the outward appearance of friendship subsisted, for the regent sent every day one of his principal officers to enquire after Captain

Dalton's health, in order to have an opportunity of discovering what he was doing. When the two months stipulated for the delivery of the city were expired, he sent four of his principal officers in form to demand the surrender of it, but Kiroodin Khan, a man haughty and insolent when no danger was near, flew out into a passion, and reproaching the commissaries with the treacherous and clandestine practices of their prince, produced the agreement with Captain Poverio, signed and sealed, and then told them plainly that they had no city to expect, but should be paid the money which the regent had disbursed, as soon as the Nabob's finances were in a better condition.

"The regent pretended to be much offended with this answer; however, after some consideration, he sent his minister to lay the accounts before the Nabob, declaring that he was willing to relinquish his claim to Trichinopoly, provided the money was immediately paid. This appearance of moderation was only intended to lessen the Nabob's character with the publick, and to justify the measures he was determined to take himself, for he was too well acquainted with his circumstances to imagine him able to pay so large a sum, which, by the accounts he produced, amounted to 8,500,000 rupees.

"There now remained little hopes of reconciling the difference, which Mr. Dupleix had from the beginning diligently influenced; knowing that it was the interest of the Morratoes to protract a war, he addressed himself particularly to Morari-row, who continually received presents and letters from him, as also from his wife. In those letters the English were represented as a plodding mercantile people, unacquainted with the art of war, and not fit to appear in the field, opposed to a nation of so martial a genius as the French, and the success at Seringham was totally ascribed to the valour and activity of the Morrattoe cavalry."*

A good idea of the general state of affairs at Trichinopoly at this time will be gained from Captain Dalton's letters to the Governor and Council at Fort St. George, the most important of which I have copied from the East India Records.

"Fort St. George, July, 1752.

"A letter from Captain Dalton telling of Morarow's double dealings, making up to both the Nabob and Rajah, and getting large sums from both. He has also offered his services to the French for 3 lacks of rupees. . . . He wants to protract the war."

---

* Orme, vol. i. pp. 259–60.

"August 3d, 1752.

"Captain Dalton writes that the differences between the King* of Mysore and Morarow have been settled, the former giving the latter a consideration of a lac of rupees, and 1,000 rupees per day to be paid by former to latter. There is reason to believe treachery is on foot between them and Mr. Dupleix."

"August 10, 1752.

"Letter from Captain Dalton at Trichinopoly saying that the Mysore King and Maratta have moved their camp from under the Fort walls to a rising ground by Warriore, which place they have demanded. Some of their troops have passed the Coleroon, and it is said with an intent to join the Nabob; if so, it is to be feared they have some treachery in view, for they are certainly in treaty with Mr. Dupleix."

"August 17th, 1752.

"Captain Dalton at Trichinopoly writes to say that the King of Mysore says Morarow was in treaty with Dupleix contrary to his inclination, but it is probable that *both* are in treaty with Dupleix."

---

* The King of Mysore constantly referred to in Captain Dalton's letters, always means the Regent, also called Rajah and Dalloway.

" August 24th, 1752.

" Letter from the Governor and Council at Fort St. George to Captain Dalton at Trichinopoly, saying it is confirmed that the King of Mysore has been in treaty with M. Dupleix, whose affairs are not satisfactory, that it is necessary to be on continual guard against treachery in Trichinopoly and keep a good eye on Gopaul Rauze. If attacked to defend fort to last extremity, and in case of any emergency, to burst all the guns and mortars, and destroy all warlike stores rather than suffer them to fall into the enemy's hands."

" August 31st, 1752.

" Letter from Captain Dalton at Trichinopoly saying 2,000 Morattoes under Innis Cawn were marching to join Nabob, and Morarow sent message to say he was very pleased Trichinopoly was not delivered up, and should never be easy to see it in the hands of the King of Mysore."

" October 9th, 1752.

" Captain Dalton at Trichinopoly writes that he had lately received a letter from the Nabob who desired him to give up the outposts, and the King having intelligence of it, had offered a bribe to comply with it, which he refused."

There are several letters from Mahommed Ali to the Governor and Council at Fort St. George. Long winded screeds explaining his past conduct and promising the English many things in the future. Every letter ended with these words—

"WHAT CAN I SAY MORE?"

If he had only said less and acted more, the English would have been better pleased!

"October 23rd, 1752.

"Captain Dalton at Trichinopoly writes that a very treacherous design to murder him (Dalton) has been discovered by the confessions of one of the Jemidars whom a Bramin from the Rajah had attempted to corrupt, on which some of the chief conspirators were seized, and are to be publicly shot *in terrorem*."

Kiroodin Khan, the Governor of Trichinopoly, did not give Captain Dalton full authority to punish civil offenders, though he left him all the responsibility of taking care of the fortress. As it was most necessary that Captain Dalton should have full power committed to him, and be able to punish civil as well as military offenders, he wrote to his commanding officer—Major Lawrence—asking him to obtain the desired permission from the Governor. Major Lawrence at once saw the necessity of this authority being granted, as the following passage in one of his letters shows:—

" Trivady, Oct. 29th, 1752.

" I must beg you fall on some method of supplying Captain Dalton with money, and please give him leave to make some examples, otherwise it's not unreasonable to imagine that the town will be lost and our people murdered.

" Signed,

" S. Lawrence.

" To the Governor and Council
at Fort St. George."

" November 6th, 1752.

" A letter to Captain Dalton at Trichinopoly from the President, approved by the Board, that in regard to such criminals as come in his own command, to act according to articles of war, as for others they come under Nabob's (Kiroodin Khan's) office, however the necessity of inflicting proper punishment should be enforced to him."

" November 13th, 1752.

" Captain Dalton at Trichinopoly writes that he is informed by his spies the Dalloway has lately received a letter from his brother advising him to return to his own country, but he declares he is determined to die rather than not return with Honour, that he will give up his pretentions to the fort if the Nabob will repay him the money he has expended; this the latter thinks unreasonable, as he requires to be paid for the expense of an army which he always keeps in his own country in peace or war. The Rajah however seems to be preparing to move, 'tis said to Caroor, and has already sent part of his baggage that way."

"November 20th, 1752.

"Captain Dalton at Trichinopoly writes that Mora-row continues to make great protestations of friendship, and says 'tis true he was in hopes of getting a sum of money from M. Dupleix, and therefore flattered him a little, but in his Heart he is attached to the Nabob's interests, and on being asked the reason of Innis Cawn leaving the Nabob, he answered there had happened a quarrel between his people and the English at Trivady, which made it necessary for them to part."

"November 27th, 1752.

"Captain Dalton at Trichinopoly writes that a Bramin and Sepoy having been sent by the Dalloway to endeavour to corrupt the Sepoys in that Fort, they had been detected in the fact, which was further proved by a writing under their hands, that Kireedi Cawn had ordered them to be executed which was accordingly done. . . . That the Rajah had lately received a present from M. Dupleix of an artificial Fig tree, the fruit of which is gold curiously wrought."

"December 8th, 1752.

"Captain Dalton at Trichinopoly writes that Morarow has taken leave of King and departed; that Kireedi Cawn says he has certain intelligence that the agreement made and sworn to before their God at Syringham, is that Morarow should not act with Nabob, but is to have a Lac and a half of Rupees to join the French, which M. Dupleix is to double."

"December 8th, 1752.

"The President writes to Captain Dalton at Trichinopoly that if Morarow (as is reported) has entered into an alliance with the French it must soon appear, and he has already written to the King of Tanjore desiring him in that case to join forces at Trichinopoly, which will disconcert their scheme, and in the meantime it is necessary to be very cautious, but on no account to be the aggressor."

No one can read the above letters without understanding the difficulty of Captain Dalton's position as Commandant of this much-coveted fortress, and the strain there must have been both on his mind and body, in observing that caution which was so continually being impressed upon him by the English authorities. It has been seen how the Regent of Mysore tried successively to assassinate, to bribe, and to surprise Captain Dalton by treachery. This treachery quite justified Major Lawrence in advising Captain Dalton to seize the persons of the Regent and Morarow, but the cautious civilian authorities at Fort St. George discountenanced the idea. This conduct on their part is thus criticised by Mr. Mill the historian :—

"The danger which might have been averted by securing the persons of those enemies was of considerable amount." *

* Mill's *History of British India*, iii. p. 129.

CHAPTER X.

(1752–1753.)

The Regent's Starvation Scheme.—Dalton ordered to treat him as an Enemy.—Marches in the Night and attacks Mysorean Camp.—Action at Seringham.—Dalton's Despatches.—He turns the 700 Mysoreans out of the City.—Weakness of the Garrison.—Famine.

THE Regent's plan was to conquer the garrison by starvation—that dread enemy which is more to be feared than a host of armed men.

The following abstract from Captain Dalton's letter to the Governor and Council at Fort St. George, refers to the Regent's attempts to starve them out.

"Fort St. George, January 5th, 1753.

"Captain Dalton at Trichinopoly writes that the Dalloway's people continue to collect all the grain about Trichinopoly to the very walls, and frequently appear in small parties with drawn swords to the great terror of the people, and even came to one of the advanced outposts, but on the Sepoys there preparing to receive them they moved off. . . . That finding he could not obtain redress from the Dalloway, he ordered the Guards at the advanced posts to fire on them if they attempted to cut the paddy,* in consequence of which there had been a little skirmish at Wycondah with a party of the enemy, wherein several of them were wounded."

The President at Fort St. George wrote in answer to Captain Dalton's letter—"that as Gopaul Rauze and 700 Peons are in Trichinopoly, if he (Captain Dalton) think it convenient, he may disarm and turn them out, which will be a good supply of spare arms, but not to part with Gopaul Rauze."

The Regent continuing to stop all provisions that were coming to the city, it was necessary to take active measures to alter this state of affairs. "The Presidency of Madrass," says Orme, "who in consideration of the Regent's pretensions to Trichinopoly, had hitherto declined to take revenge of his treacherous attempts to get possession of it, now thought it time to treat him as a declared enemy.

"In consequence of this resolution, Captain Dalton

* Rice in the husk.

on the 23rd of December, marched out of the city at ten o'clock at night with the greatest part of the Europeans and Sepoys to beat up his camp, which extended under the northern wall of Seringham; but the Regent himself with a considerable guard remained within the pagoda. An artillery officer with three pieces of cannon was previously posted on the southern bank of the Caveri, opposite the pagoda, with orders to create what alarm he could by throwing shot into the place as soon as he should hear the fire of the musketry in the camp. The troops passed the Caveri at Chuckley-pollam, and then crossing the island marched along the bank of the Coleroon, until they came within a quarter of a mile of the enemy's camp, where they halted in order to refresh themselves and to form for the attack; but on the review it was found that no less than 500 of the Sepoys were absent, having, as they afterwards affirmed, inadvertently missed the line of march in the dark; however, the rest not appearing discouraged it was determined to proceed. They were divided into two distinct bodies, and they first marched only four in front, being designed to penetrate through the camp, firing two to the right and two to the left; whilst the others drawn up in a more compact manner, were ordered to halt as soon as they came amongst the tents, and there remain as a support to the first party, who moving on found the enemy's advanced guard fast asleep, and stabbing them with their bayonets entered the camp without opposition, and to the right and left began a brisk fire from front to rear. The alarm was instantly spread and produced such consternation that nothing was heard but the shrieks of men wounded, and the outcries of others warning their friends to fly from their danger. The enemy according to their senseless custom raised a number of blue lights in the air, in order to discover the motions of the column, but these lights served much better to direct the fire against themselves; in the meantime those within the pagoda manned the walls, but refrained from firing for fear of killing their own people in the camp, who in less than an hour were totally dispersed, and if the English had brought with them a petard, they would probably have forced into the pagoda, and have finished the war by securing the person of the Regent. Everything being now quiet, the Sepoys were permitted to take as many horses as they could conveniently lead away, and marching foremost out of the camp were followed by the Europeans in good order; but by this time, the Mysoreans within the pagoda, finding by the extinction of the lights that none of their own army remained within reach, began to fire smartly from the walls, and killed and wounded twenty men, of whom seven were Europeans.

"The troops reached the city by daybreak, when they discovered the enemy returning to the island, who immediately struck all their tents and retired into the pagoda. This sufficiently showed their panic, but nevertheless it was evident that their continuance in the neighbourhood would prevent the inhabitants from bringing in provisions, of which they began already to feel the want. Captain Dalton therefore determined to bombard the pagoda, not doubting that if he could drive the enemy out of it, their fears would deter them from encamping again within a night's march." *

The above events are chronicled in the *East India Records* as follows :—

"Fort St. George, Jan. 15, 1753.

"Captain Dalton at Trichinopoly writes that in order to keep his Sepoys in readiness—he having found it necessary to encamp without the town—the Raja was much alarmed, and sent Kireedi Cawn word he would recall Morarirow, but when it came to the point he decided he would do it only in case the Nabob would give him the Fort or a Crore of Rupees, that thereupon, and having at the same time received certain

* Vol. i. pp. 268–9

intelligence of the hostilities committed by Morarirow, he, at Kireedi Cawn's request, determined to make an attack on the Mysorean camp, and accordingly after leaving a sufficient security for the garrison, marched in the night, and although 500 of his Sepoys missed their way in the dark, yet with the rest of his men he attacked camp with such vigour and success, that in less than three-quarters of an hour they were entire masters of it, having lost but one European and 2 Sepoys wounded; that during the whole action his military behaved with great coolness, and never offered to plunder. . . . The Sepoys took a great number of horses, firelocks, and as much plunder as they could carry off. That upon this success he resolved to bombard Syringham the following night, the events of which he relates in the following letter :—

"Trichinopoly,

"Jan. 5th, 1753.

"Sir,

"In my last I gave you an account of our havin routed the Raja and Morarirow's camp in the night, and of their having sheltered themselves within the walls, in consequence of which last night I resolved to bombard 'em, and accordingly attacked a Choultry within 600 yards of the place, which we easily carried, and having Coolys, &c. ready, immediately intrenched the part of it that was open, with a strong wall, and put a company of Sepoys on the top of it.

"I think it was as strong a post as ever I saw, and we all thought it as safe as Trichinopoly. When I had regulated everything, I left Lieuts. Wilkey and Crow there with 70 military and 300 Sepoys, and Lieut. Wood with a 12-pounder and a half-pound gun. For still the greater security I lodged myself with the remains of my command and two field pieces within point blank shot to support them.

"The enemy appeared out of the pagoda and made a push with their Sepoys at the choultry, but were repulsed with great ease and no small slaughter. They came again however about 12 o'clock, with their whole force horse and foot all round. The bloodiest action ensued that I believe has ever been seen in this part of the world, for they had intoxicated their people with bang, and they rode on very surprisingly; wever, as their horse made the boldest attack, and I g sure the post was in no danger from them, we kept very hot fire on them and repulsed 'em twice, leaving the ground strewn with their dead. Notwithstanding this they made a third charge, and our rascally Sepoys gave way, which discouraged the Europeans so much that tho' they had but 2 or 3 wounded and close intrenched, they quitted their officers, and ran out of the post, the natural consequence of which was that the horse instantly charged 'em in their disorder, and killed or wounded almost the whole, notwithstanding the fire of my party.

"Encouraged by their success they made a vigorous push at my party, but I had rally'd the Sepoys and placed 'em behind a little wall to receive them, and we sent them off in great confusion. They rally'd again, and came up with great fury, calling us all the names they could invent, but my grape shot annoyed 'em so much, joined to our continual fire of musketry, that they were obliged to retreat and we kept our ground. The native horse of which we had about 40, galloped a little way after them, and took the horses of those that were killed. The Raja has just now sent word that he desires a cessation of arms that both partys may bury their dead, of which there's more than ever I saw in my life all put together.

"You easily perceive, Sir, that if my people had not so imprudently quitted their post we had gained a complete victory. These are accidents mankind can't foresee. With regard to myself I leave the Nabob who was a spectator from the wall, and public report, to satisfy you of my management and what efforts I made.

"Lieuts. Wilkey and Crow with about 60 men as near as I can compute are missing. When the enemy retreated I brought off the wounded, in all about 19 men with Lieut. Wood,* who I hope will do well.

"I will send you particular returns to-morrow as well of the military as Sepoys, of the latter in the whole action I believe we have near a 100 missing. The enemy themselves own 9 jemidars and 300 men killed, besides numbers wounded. The Nabob says they have lost above 800 men and I really can't see how it could be otherwise.

"Since the action no hostilities have been committed on either side.

"The Dalloway has wrote the Nabob a sort of palavering letter in which he says he had best] be friends. I have turned out the Mysorean peons, and the Killedar has a guard over Gopaul Rauze, so that all is quite easy within; I sent the peons out with their arms, baggage, and everything that belonged to them.

"I am, Sir,

"Yr very obedient servant,

"JOHN DALTON.

"To the Hon. Thos. Saunders, Esq."

---

* Lieutenant Wood died shortly afterwards from his wounds, and so great was the scarcity of officers at Trichinopoly, that a lieute-

No one can read Captain Dalton's despatches without seeing how studiously he avoids the subject of "self." This modesty is all the more to be admired because it is rare. Public report was more likely to do justice to Captain Dalton's good management during the above spirited engagement, than the Governor, who remained on the city walls, at a safe distance during the fighting.

The real cause of the panic which ended so disastrously for the Europeans and Sepoys who were left to guard the choultry, is explained by Orme in his account of the engagement—"The Morattoes," says this writer, "encouraged by this success* now galloped up to the entrenchment of the great choultry, where they were suffered to come so near, that several of them made use of their sabres across the parapet before the troops within gave fire, which then began, and seconded by that of the four pieces of cannon on the other side of the river, killed and wounded a great number of men and horses and obliged the enemy to retire in confusion; in this instant an officer unadvisedly took

---

nant's commission was given to Sergeant Dickinson who had distinguished himself.—*East India Records.*

* Referring to a body of the Nabob's sepoys having been driven from a small choultry of which they had taken possession, and put to flight by a body of Mahrattas.—Orme, vol. i. p. 270.

the resolution of quitting his post, and passed the river in order to give Captain Dalton some information concerning the artillery; some of the soldiers seeing this imagined he went away through fear, and concluding that things were worse than appeared to them, followed his example and ran out of the entrenchment, which the rest perceiving, a panic seized the whole, and they left the post with the greatest precipitation, notwithstanding they had the minute before given three huzzas, on the retreat of the Morattoes."

The unfortunate mistake that this officer made in quitting his post caused this unforeseen catastrophe. Captain Dalton was of too generous a nature to mention this in his despatches, as the officer had only acted in excessive zeal, as his commander was well aware.

"This disaster," continues Orme, "diminished the strength of the garrison near one half, not by the number, but by the quality of the troops that were lost." *

The Governor at Fort St. George on receipt of

---

* Lieutenants Wilkey and Crow having vainly endeavoured to rally their men, gallantly determined to stay in the entrenchment, where they were cut to pieces.—Orme, vol. i. p. 271.

Captain Dalton's despatch wrote at once to him, urging him to be "most cautious in all his undertakings and not run any risk." At the same time he blamed Captain Dalton for having allowed the 700 Mysoreans to depart with their arms and baggage. It may be thought that this generosity on the part of the Commandant was ill-timed, but, setting aside the idea that all is fair in war, the laws of honour seemed to forbid the despoiling of these Mysoreans, who had been received into the city as hostages, and could not be held answerable for the bad faith and treacherous conduct of the Regent.

The following extract from Orme informs us of the events that followed the late engagements :—

"Lest the enemy should imagine that he was totally dispirited if he should remain inactive, Captain Dalton determined to make some attempt, which at the same time that it might be executed without much risque, might make them believe he was still in a capacity to act in the field. They had a post about four miles west of Trichinopoly at a pagoda called Velore, where the guard prevented the country people from carrying provisions into the city. The pagoda had a strong stone wall, and they had choked up the great gate with mud, leaving at the bottom a wicket, by which only one man could enter at a time, and this they carefully shut every evening. Thirty Europeans marched in a dark night, and having concealed themselves in a watercourse near the gate, a sergeant of artillery, caring a barrel of gunpowder with a long sausage to it went forward and digging, placed the barrel under the wicket unobserved, although the centinel was sitting at the top of the gate singing a Moorish song. The explosion not only brought down the mud work, but also blew up the terrace of the gateway with the guard asleep on it, so that the soldiers entered immediately without difficulty, and, having fresh in their memory the loss of their comrades at the choultry, put all the Mysoreans they met to the sword.

"The Regent, convinced by this exploit that famine would be the surest means of reducing the garrison, ordered a party of 200 horse to lie on the plain every night between the city and the country of the Polygor Tondeman, from whence alone provisions were obtained. They seized some of the people bringing in rice, and according to their barbarous custom cut off their noses, and sent them thus mangled to Trichinopoly. This cruelty struck such a terror that for some days no one would venture to bring in supplies. In order therefore to dislodge this detachment 400 men, Sepoys and Europeans, with two field-pieces, marched in the evening, and took possession of the ground where they used to pass the night; the enemy coming up some time after, did not discover their danger before they received the fire of the troops, which immediately put them to flight, and by their outcries it was imagined they suffered considerably.

"Whatever might be their loss, the surprize struck such a terror, that no more small detachments could be prevailed on to remain within reach of the garrison during the dark nights; and their refusal suggested to the Regent the resolution of dividing his force, and forming a considerable camp between the city and Tondeman's country, whilst he remained with the rest at Seringham. A multitude of people set to the work finished in a few days an entrenchment, with a stout mud wall, at a place called Facquire's *Tope*, or the grove of the Facquire, situated four miles to the south, and one to the west of the city, after which 5,000 horse and 3,000 foot, being nearly one-half of the army, and the best troops in it, moved from the island with their baggage, and pitched their tents within this fortification. The effect of this disposition was soon severely felt; no more grain was brought to the market, the shops were shut, and the inhabitants began to cry famine, whilst the garrison had the mortification to perceive themselves incapable of removing the distress, being, since the loss at the choultry, too weak to cope with the enemy in either of their camps.

"Such was the situation of affairs at Trichinopoly at the end of March, 1753."*

At this crisis in the Company's affairs, Captain Robert Clive was compelled, by ill-health, to return to England. He sailed for England in March, on board the "Bombay Castle," immediately after his marriage at Madras to Miss Margaret Maskelyne—sister of his friend Captain Edmund Maskelyne. One of the homeward-bound passengers in the same ship with the bride and bridegroom was Robert Orme, the future Indian historian.

---

* Vol. i. pp. 272–73; Dalton's *Journal*, fos. 126–28.

CHAPTER XI.

Lawrence's Despatch to the Governor and Council.—Startling Discovery made by Dalton at Trichinopoly.—His Despatch to Lawrence at Trivadi —Lawrence marches with his whole Force to Trichinopoly.—Dalton cannonades the Mysorean Camp and captures Baggage and Grain.—Battle of the Golden Rock.—Mahommed Ali insulted by his Troops in Trichinopoly, and not allowed to leave his Palace.—Is rescued by Dalton and escorted to Lawrence's Camp by the Grenadier Company.—Famine Prices in Trichinopoly.—The French Spy—Is detected by Dalton, who tries to entrap the French in their own Toils.—Lawrence arrives with Provisions.—Second Battle of the Golden Rock.—Execution of the French Spy.—Battle of the Sugar-Loaf Hill.

THE European garrison of Trichinopoly was reduced to a mere handful of men, and the Commandant was quite unable to risk any more sorties against the enemy. The city was strongly blockaded by the Regent's army, and all means of obtaining provisions from the surrounding country were now cut off. The Governor and Council at Fort St. George were quite aware of the danger Trichinopoly was in, but they took no immediate steps to send a relieving party there.

While these affairs were taking place at Trichinopoly, Major Lawrence with the troops under his command were engaged in opposing the French on the sea-coast.

"Mr. Dupleix," says Orme, "whose eye was always on Trichinopoly, determined to protract the war on the sea coast as long as possible, that the Mysoreans might not be interrupted from blockading the city."

Major Lawrence, with that promptness of action which so often distinguishes the military from the civil authority, saw the absolute necessity of sending relief to Captain Dalton, and wrote to the Governor and Council in the straightforward manner which was characteristic of this gallant commander. The following extract from his letter refers to Captain Dalton's position:—

"Trivady Camp, April 19th, 1753.

"If Captain Dalton is to be reinforced, and his situation seems to cry aloud for it, 'tis high time to determine something, for the rising of the rivers (and that season is approaching) will put it out of our power to assist him."*

The date of this letter must be particularly noticed,

---

* *East India Records.*

as the day after, Major Lawrence received a despatch from Captain Dalton, which made all further delay impossible. Before giving a copy of this despatch, I must relate what had taken place at Trichinopoly early in April.

"Captain Dalton," says Colonel Wilks, "had frequently communicated with Kheir a Deen on the subject of the question of the quantities (of provisions) in store, and was always assured they were abundant, but now that these stores were to be his only resource, he prudently insisted on examining them himself, and establish such arrangements for their issue and expenditure, as should satisfy his mind with regard to his actual situation and means of sustaining the blockade."

Captain Dalton had often been assured by the Governor of Trichinopoly that there were enough provisions for four months, instead of which there were hardly any left at all.

"Captain Dalton," says Orme, "insisted on examining the magazines, when to his great surprize Kiroodin Khan informed him that he had taken advantage of the scarcity, to sell out the provisions to the inhabitants at a high price, not doubting but that opportunities of replacing them would offer, and acknowledged that the stock remaining was no more than sufficient for 15 days—in which time the army at Trivadi could hardly receive the news, and march to the relief of the city. Expostulations were vain, for the mischief was real; an express was therefore sent with this alarming intelligence to Major Lawrence, who received it at ten at night the 20th of April."*

Captain Dalton's despatch to Major Lawrence is given at length in the East India Records for 1753, and is as follows:—

"Trichinopoly, April 13th, 1753.

"DEAR MAJOR,

"I wrote you lately several letters that by the present situation of the enemy, we are so blockaded that not the least provisions of any sort can possibly come into the fort. They keep likewise at such a vast distance that there is no possibility of interrupting them. They never now since they attacked our advanced post appear within cannon shot. Kiroodi Cawn has been often pressing me to write to you to come this way, which I imputed to his fears as he is a timorous man, but last night he sent for Mr. Harrison and me, and protested to us before God that there was now but 20 days provisions for the garrison within the walls, and that if you don't speedily march

* Vol. i. p. 280; Dalton's *Journal*, fo. 129.

this way all will be ruined. I have always been very cautious of applying to you on that head, lest such a movement might prejudice your affairs; but as things now stand, and Kiroodi Cawn having likewise apply'd to me in writing, which is I suppose to throw the blame of what may happen off himself, it is to be sure my duty to acquaint you of it, particularly as it is an affair of the utmost consequence. It is but a month ago that I demanded of him in the Governor's name what quantity of provisions were in the garrison, and he assured me of 4 months at least; what interest he could have in deceiving me I can't conceive. There is so little time now to spare that your sending a detachment would not answer. The enemy will inevitably endeavour if not to stop them at least considerably detain them on the road. I am persuaded that if on the receipt of this you only make a couple of marches this way, the Raja will instantly decamp, for he trembles at your name, and should he stay till you arrive at Semiveram, we can soon despatch him between two fires, tho' I am very certain that before you arrive at Volconda, he will be far from Caroor. The shortness of our provisions which the Nabob* till now always kept a secret to me is a *thunderclap at this juncture,*

* Meaning Kiroodin Khan.

however it is exactly the *state of affairs* as he has reported to us and under his seal, and I could not avoid referring it to you as it is of the *utmost consequence*, and I am persuaded you 'l take the necessary steps to assist us. With regard to my Europeans, we can make 40 shifts, but the black fellows will all decamp the first day they want their rice.

"I am,

"Your most obedt. very humble servant,

"JOHN DALTON.

"Since I wrote the above, the Nabob has been at me again to solicit you to arrive here *before* 15 *days from the date of this*. I have already said all he told me on this subject, and can only assure you that whatever distress we are driven to, you'l find that while I have life I will not render myself unworthy of my charge.

"To Major Lawrence,

"Trivadi."

We already know when this despatch reached Major Lawrence, and the thread of our narrative is now continued in that gallant commander's own words :—*

"Astonished at this intelligence we saw the neces-

* Lawrence's Narrative in Cambridge's *History*, p 43.

sity of an immediate march to Trichinopoly, which we began the 22nd instant in the morning, leaving Captain Chase with 150 Europeans and 500 Sepoys for the defence of Trivady, and as I intended passing thro' the Tanjore country, letters were despatched by the Nabob and me to the King acquainting him with our march, and inviting him to join us on our approach to his capital. Tho' we proceeded as expeditiously as possible we were obliged to halt every 3rd or 4th day on account of the hot winds, which were so powerful at this season that notwithstanding all our care our little army was greatly diminished. We marched by Chillambrum a strong pagoda in which we had a sergeant and a few gunners. A place of so much consequence for preserving our communication by land between St. David's and the Tanjore country should have been reinforced; instead of that our men were withdrawn, and it fell into the enemy's hands soon after our departure. On our entering the Tanjore country the King sent his prime minister Succogee to compliment the Nabob and his allies. He received our force and promised very fairly on the part of his master to whom he soon afterwards returned. We pursued our march to Condore the 3d of May. On our arrival the King desired to meet the Nabob and me half way. I set out the 4th in company with the Nabob and Mr. Palk, who had been with me from my leaving Madras. The King met us at the place appointed attended by his whole court, who on the occasion made a very magnificent and splendid appearance. He was escorted by 3,000 horse well mounted, and a great many elephants in silver trappings. After ceremoniously passing each other in our palankeens, we were conducted to a pleasant garden, and there received by the King under a pavillion supported by pillars of silver elegantly covered and furnished. There we renewed our assurances of friendship and protection, and all our former engagements, and it was determined that the King should support the Nabob, and join him the next day with 3,000 horse, and a like number of Sepoys. After a refreshment of fruits, a shower of rose water, and being anointed with atter of roses, we were dismissed with presents of elephants, horses, and sirpahs,* and escorted to our camp by a brilliant party of the Raja's cavalry.

"On the 5th the horse and Sepoys joined us according to agreement, but, as we soon after experienced, only to make a parade, for they left us the same day. We arrived the 6th May at Trichinopoly."

---

* Garments presented sometimes by superiors in token of protection, and sometimes by inferiors in token of homage.—Orme, p. 159.

In the meantime Captain Dalton had not been idle at Trichinopoly. What measures the Commandant took to harass the enemy, are given in the following extracts from the *Records of the First Madras European Regiment,** which was the name afterwards given to the English battalion at this time commanded by Lawrence—this battalion then including the Artillery, the troop of Cavalry, and the Grenadier company :—

"In the meantime Dalton, at Trichinopoly, had not been inactive in annoying the enemy and procuring small supplies of provisions for the daily consumption of his garrison. Knowing the Mysore general, who commanded the force in the intrenched camp at the Faqueer's Tope, to be a very timid man in night attacks, he determined by frequent annoyances, to drive him from his position, and thus on one side of the city, open the blockade. To effect this, a redoubt near the city, and within random shot of the enemy, was thrown up, and two pieces of heavy cannon mounted in it. This post having been well secured, the guard frequently sallied out at night with two field-pieces and fired grape into the Mysore camp, returning with their guns in the morning. The enemy never

---

* *Historical Records of the First Madras European Regiment,* by a Staff Officer.

once attempted to intercept them ; and encouraged by their timidity, on the night of the 15th of April they fired thirty rounds of grape, at a short range from each of the field pieces into the camp. The execution was so severe, that the enemy abandoned their camp in no little hurry and confusion the following morning, and joined the rest of the investing army at Seringam. The country people were thus induced to supply the garrison with abundance of provisions, and on entering the deserted camp a quantity of baggage and a large quantity of grain was found and carried into the city.

" On the 6th of May Lawrence entered Trichinopoly with his convoy, but he had failed in procuring the Tanjore cavalry, and the number of his Europeans from the great heat had been sadly diminished by deaths on the march ; desertions had also taken place from the Swiss company, and 100 sick were carried into the city. The effective state, therefore, of the whole corps for field duty, including what the garrison could spare, was only 500 Europeans, 80 artillerymen, 2,000 sepoys and 3,000 of the Nabob's rabble of cavalry. The day after the English arrived, a reinforcement of 200 French, with four field-pieces, and 500 Sepoys joined the Mysoreans at Seringam."

Captain Dalton being left to keep guard over Trichinopoly, did not share in Lawrence's actions with the enemy, who had been further reinforced by 300 French soldiers and 1,000 Sepoys. Lawrence's force was very inferior in point of numbers, but knowing that the fate of Trichinopoly depended on his gaining a victory over the enemy, he determined to seek an engagement. On June 26th was fought the battle of the Golden Rock (a small post north-east of Trichinopoly), in which Lawrence gained a most complete victory over the French and their allies.

"Thus," says Orme, "was Trichinopoly saved by a success which astonished even those who had gained it; nor was the attempt, however desperate it might seem, justified by the success alone, for as the city would inevitably have fallen if the English had remained inactive, so the loss of it would have been hastened only a few days if they had been defeated, and Major Lawrence acted with as much sagacity as spirit, in risquing everything to gain a victory on which alone depended the preservation of the great object of the war."

After this success Lawrence determined to avoid another engagement, until he had been joined by some troops just arrived from Europe. Being in want of cavalry, he determined to march into the Tanjore country and make renewed efforts to induce the King of Tanjore to furnish him with some cavalry, which had been before promised. "The presence of the Nabob," says Orme, "being thought necessary to facilitate the negotiation, he prepared to march with the army, but on the evening that he intended to quit the city, his discontented troops assembled in the outer court of the palace, and clamouring declared they would not suffer him to move, before he had paid their arrears; in vain were arguments to convince this rabble, more insolent because they had never rendered any essential service, that his going to Tanjore was the only measure for which they could hope for a chance of receiving their pay; they remained inflexible, and threatened violence, upon which Captain Dalton sent a message to the camp, from whence the grenadier company immediately marched into the city, where they were joined by a hundred of the garrison, and all together forcing their way into the palace, they got the Nabob into his palankeen, and escorted him to the camp surrounded by 200 Europeans with fixed bayonets."

On July 2, Lawrence marched to Tanjore accompanied by the Nabob and fifty. of his cavalry.

"The rest of the Nabob's cavalry," says Orme, "remained encamped under the walls of Trichinopoly, and a few days after the departure of the English army went in a body, and informed Captain Dalton that they intended to go over to the enemy, with whom they had made their terms, desiring at the same time that he would not fire upon them as they were marching off. This, as he was very glad to get rid of such a dangerous encumbrance, he readily promised, and they went away unmolested at noonday.

"The enemy having now no other immediate object gave their whole attention to blockade the city, which they were in a condition to effect without much difficulty; for their superiority in Europeans deterred the garrison from venturing without the walls to interrupt their night patroles, as was their custom when they had only the Mysoreans and Morattoes to encounter. However, Captain Dalton took the precaution of undermining in a dark night the posts of Warriore and Weycondah to the west of the city; the defences of Warriore were ruined, but the explosion failed at Weycondah.

"The late supplies of provisions being entirely reserved for the use of the garrison, the inhabitants were left to provide for themselves, and rice was now sold in the market for half-a-crown the measure, about an English quart, which was fifteen times dearer than the common price, and firewood was scarcely to be procured at any rate. This scarcity soon obliged them to quit their habitations, and in less than a month this spacious city, which had formerly contained 400,000 persons, was left almost desolate; for the military people who remained in it, soldiers and artificers of all denominations, did not exceed 2,000 men. Of these the Nabob's Peans, as being capable of no other service than to give an alarm, were posted between the outward and inward wall; their number was about 1,000; the Sepoys, 600, were stationed round the ramparts, and the Europeans, about 200, were appointed some to guard the gates, whilst the rest lay on their arms every night in readiness to march to any quarter where the alarm might be given."*

I said before that it required the hundred eyes of Argus to detect all the schemes that were planned for the capture of Trichinopoly, and I now make the remark again with renewed assurance of its truth. The Regent, with his dull brain, had concocted some very well-planned schemes; but a master mind had now set to work to capture by strategy the coveted fortress of the Carnatic. The master mind belonged to Dupleix—that despot who astonished even the Native Princes by his craftiness, unscrupulousness, and bombastic love of display.

Vol. i. pp. 296-97; Dalton's *Journal*, fol. 142, &c.

"Mr. Dupleix," says Orme, quoting from Dalton's *Journal*, "strenuously importuned Mr. Brenier, who had succeeded Mr. Astruc in the command, to attempt an escalade at all events, and suggested to him a method of getting the information he wanted by sending one De Cattans, an intelligent officer, as a deserter into the town; the man was promised the command of a company and 30,000 rupees, for which he not only undertook to find out the proper spot where they should place their scaling-ladders, but also to maintain a correspondence with the French prisoners, who were to break loose and seize the arms of the guard, and attack the quarters of the English whilst the assault was made on the walls. He was admitted into the city, and said that he came into the city to offer his service to the English, being disgusted by an unjust censure which had been cast on his conduct in the late battle at the Golden Rock; an overstrained affectation of frankness in his behaviour gave Captain Dalton some suspicions, and two spies were set to watch his actions, who at different times discovered him measuring the calibre of the guns, taking a survey of the works, and fathoming the height of the wall with a lead and line, after which he threw notes through the windows to the French prisoners. There was in the garrison a French soldier whose fidelity to the English might be depended on; this man engaged to detect his countryman still more effectually, and suffered himself to be chastized in his sight by Captain Dalton for some pretended neglect, after which he affected such a resentment for this treatment, that De Cattans gave him his entire confidence, offering him a great reward if he would assist in the execution of his plan. The soldier said he was not made for great enterprizes, but offered to desert the first night he should be on guard at the barrier, and to carry a letter, provided De Cattans would assure him of a pardon for having deserted from the French. This the other readily agreed to, and gave him a pardon in form signed with his name, to which he added the title of 'plenipotentiary of the Marquis Dupleix.' At the same time he delivered to him a letter for Mr. Brenier, which contained a full and exact description of the defences of the place, and some commendations on his own address in deceiving the English commandant, whom he described as a very young man, that placed more confidence in him than in any of his own officers. The soldier carried the letter to Captain Dalton, who immediately caused De Cattans to be arrested; at first he denied the fact, but on seeing his own writing, desired that he might not suffer the disgrace of being hanged, but have the honour of being shot by a file of musketeers. He was told his fate could not be decided before Major Lawrence arrived; Captain Dalton, however, desirous of drawing the enemy into a snare by the same means which they had employed against himself, promised the criminal to intercede for his pardon, provided he would write a letter to Mr. Brenier and prevail upon him to attempt an escalade at such a part as he, Captain Dalton, should dictate. This De Cattans readily agreed to; the place fixed upon was Dalton's battery, on the west side, not far from the northern angle, as being more accessible than any other from without, but the defences and entrenchments within were stronger than anywhere else. A black fellow undertook to carry the letter for eight rupees, and Mr. Brenier, giving him twenty, sent him back with a letter to De Cattans, promising to put his plan into execution, and desiring him to write frequently. In vain did the garrison watch several nights successively, hoping that the enemy would make the assault; but the various reports which they received of Major Lawrence's arrival kept them in such a continual bustle and alarm that they could not spare a night for the execution of this enterprizé, notwithstanding they appeared convinced of its practicability.

"The Mysoreans, finding that the explosion made

at Weycondah had done little damage, took possession of this post, and mounting two small pieces of cannon on the rampart, encamped 300 horse and some Peans under the walls, and as the garrison of Trichinopoly had not lately ventured into the field, those troops slept in perfect security without a single centinel. Captain Dalton, receiving intelligence of their negligence, resolved to beat up their quarters, and chusing a time when it was very dark, a party of 400 men, mostly Sepoys, marched up close to the tents, and made a general discharge amongst them before they were once challenged. The Sepoys got some horses and arms, and the whole party retreated out of reach before the enemy were sufficiently rouzed to do more than fire a few shots at random. At length, after remaining a month closely blockaded, and obliged to be continually on their guard, the garrison received advice that the Major was approaching. . . . On the 7th of August the army arrived at Dalaway's choultry situated close to the southern bank of the Caveri, six miles east of Trichinopoly."

The Major was bringing a convoy of some thousands of bullocks laden with provisions, Trichinopoly being in distress for food. The French and Mysoreans were very anxious to prevent these provisions from reaching the city, and prepared to engage Lawrence's force as soon as it should appear. Captain Dalton was enabled to inform the Major's force of the enemy's intentions by means of signals from the observatory on the top of Trichinopoly Rock. This rock is thus described in Lawrence's narrative :—

" A most extraordinary rock stands in the middle of the old town, and is about 300 feet high. On the top of it is a pagoda, which was of singular use to us the whole war, its height commanding even as far as Tanjore, which is 40 miles. Here was constantly stationed a man with a telescope, who gave us by signals and writing an account of all the enemy's motions."

Lawrence, continuing his march, discovered the enemy drawn up in force in a strong position extending from the French to the Golden Rock. An action was unavoidable, and what is known as the second battle of the Golden Rock took place. The only part that Captain Dalton was able to take in it was to sally from the city with two field-pieces, and increase the disorder of the enemy by attacking them in the rear. This is made mention of by Orme, as follows :—

" The English battalion was drawn up in the open plain without shelter, and in this situation suffered considerably, whilst their artillery did little mischief to the enemy; however the shot that flew over the bank went amongst a large body of horse who were drawn up in the rear of the advanced party, and flung them into confusion, which Captain Dalton observing, he sallied from the city with two field-pieces, and the cavalry, finding themselves between two fires, hurried out of reach, some to the east, and others to the west."

The Grenadiers—Captain Dalton's old Company—particularly distinguished themselves in this battle. They lost their Captain (Kirk) during the fight, and Captain Kilpatrick, putting himself at their head, exhorted them to follow him and revenge their leader's death, which they swore with an oath to do.*

"In this temper," says Orme, "they pushed on, and in order to prevent the enemy from retreating to their main body, marched to gain their right flank; the enemy had not the courage to stand the shock, but quitted the bank in great precipitation, and leaving three field-pieces behind them, ran away towards Weycondah, exposed great part of the way to the fire of the two field-pieces which Captain Dalton had brought out of the city, every shot of which for several discharges, took off two or three men."

The enemy being entirely routed, the much-needed

---

* Lawrence's Narrative, p. 50.

provisions were brought into the city, and two days after Lawrence marched out with the English battalion and the allies. Before he left he ordered De Cattans to be hanged in sight of the enemy's advanced guards.

"He died," says Orme, "with great resolution, but showed much concern that he had endeavoured to betray Captain Dalton, who had received him with so much hospitality and kindness. As the English had condescended to employ this delinquent against his own countrymen, after he was detected, his life ought to have been spared."

I am very sure his life would have been spared, if the Commandant—"the very young man," as the spy slightingly termed him—could have obtained his pardon; but Lawrence saw the absolute necessity of making an example, and putting a stop to those underhand plots which had so often endangered the safety of the fortress and the lives of the garrison.

Dupleix, in his *Memoirs,* complains with great bitterness that, excepting Bussy, he never had an officer on whose ability he could place the smallest reliance; * but even supposing this to be true, the French were much stronger in native and European

---

* Mill's *History of British India*, iii. p. 130.

allies than the British, and two such men as Dupleix and Bussy were, in their respective ways, worth a host of armed men.

On September 21, Lawrence gained another decisive victory over the French and their allies. This action was called the battle of the Sugar Loaf Rock. The following extracts from the *Records of the First Madras European Regiment* show the decisive nature of this victory. "The left wing of English Sepoys having pushed on outside the entrenched works to the right of the French regiment, attacked the Sugar Loaf Hill, and carried it in gallant style, keeping up a heavy fire on the masses running about the Mahratta and Mysore camp. During this time the regiment had formed a line to the front on its leading division, and advanced briskly towards the French battalion. Captain Kilpatrick was on this occasion severely wounded. . . . Captain Calliaud,* who had succeeded Kilpatrick in command of the Grenadiers, observing the flank of the French regiment exposed, from the flight of their Sepoys, wheeled rapidly to his left, charged in upon it, and after a very short *melée* drove them in confusion upon their centre; the other two divisions

---

* A future Commandant of Trichinopoly. He died a Major-General.

advancing at the same time at the charge, completed the rout, and the enemy broke and fled. . . . The enemy were defeated at all points and abandoned their camp, leaving their tents standing, and all their artillery (eleven pieces), ammunition and baggage. . . . In addition to the prisoners taken during the action, about 200 of the French battalion were picked up or killed wandering in Tondiman's and the Tanjore country; and after the action, whilst they were passing towards Seringam, Dalton sallied out from Trichinopoly and captured nearly thirty, making a total loss in prisoners to the French regiment of about 300 men. . . . On the following day the force marched and encamped at the French Rock, and an officer was dispatched to the King of Tanjore to hasten the supply of provisions, who succeeded in part, and a three months' supply was laid up in Trichinopoly."

CHAPTER XII.

(1753–1754.)

Private Letters.—Dalton applies to be relieved from the Command of Trichinopoly.—His Resignation not accepted.—Ill-health the Cause of his Request.—His Letter to the Council at Fort St. George.—Their Reply.—Dalton's own Account of his Departure from Trichinopoly.—Volunteers to relieve Palam Cotah.—Night Attack on Trichinopoly by the French.—Dalton's Battery described.—Result of the Attack.—Dalton resigns his Commission March 1st, 1754.—Is thanked by the Governor and Council for his Services.—Sails for England March 10.

TIME'S destroying hand has left only one or two of Captain Dalton's private letters to throw any additional light on his military career. There is, however, one letter written from the camp near Trichinopoly, in April 1752, which contains several items of interest. This letter, the address of which is lost, appears to have been written to Captain Lancelot Baugh* of the 41st Regiment, or Invalids, who had

* This officer served many years in the 1st Foot Guards, and attained the rank of captain April 18, 1743. On July 22, 1751, he was transferred to the 41st Regiment, then styled "The Invalids,"

some connections, either on his own or on his wife's side, at Limerick,* and was personally acquainted with Mrs. James Dalton before her widowhood. He had served for some years in the 6th Regiment as an ensign. He was a most kind friend to the desolate widow during her son's long absence in India, when she was left stranded in England, far from her own relatives and friends. The letter to Captain Baugh is as follows :—

"DEAR SIR,

"I am favoured with yours by ye Dorrington, accompany'd with four letters from my mother; you realy, Sir, lay me continually under such a number of repeated obligations that I am quite at a loss for words to express my gratitude; you have acted like a father to both me and my mother. How greatly it shocks me when I think how greatly that poor woman must have been distressed at my long silence, but Providence was most kind in granting her a friend of your honour

---

probably from being composed of old officers invalided from other regiments. He resided at Portsmouth, and died senior captain of his regiment in 1775.

* Lieut.-General Lancelot Baugh (eldest son of Captain Lancelot Baugh), Colonel of the 6th Regiment of Foot, who died in April, 1792, and whose will was proved in the following June, left a legacy *to his cousin Mrs. Charles Hill of Limerick.*

and humanity. Believe me, Dear Sir, I shall to ye last hour of my life retain a just sense of all your friendly favours to her, and proclaim your disinterested worth as long as I have breath to doe it. I am infinitely obliged to you for your paternal advice, in consequence of which I shall not in a hurry quit ye service I am in, which by all accounts is far preferable to ye King's; it is true we are always in Camp and run some little risques, but I may venture to assure you that I have at this time little less than forty shillings per day, and had yesterday a prest. of a fine horse worth 100 pounds at least, for taking one of ye Enemy's field pieces with my Grenadiers. These things you know seldom happen in Europe, notwithstanding which I confess to you that I am so fond a son, that I can hardly reconcile myself to staying longer from my Dear Mother, and am not ashamed to own it neither.

"I am now worth £6,000 at least, and have a very fair prospect of augmenting it considerably, and think I may venture home with ten thousand pounds in my pocket, for If I goe into ye army again, it shall be into ye Horse Service, for I can't bear ye thought of leaving England again suddenly after ye long time I have been out of it. I have not seen Fort St. David's these 14 months; wee have been continually in camp which has put it out of my power to execute Mrs. Baugh's commission, but intend soon to quit ye field for a month, when I shall take care to do it in ye best manner I am capable of, and also send her whatever I can meet with, that I think will be acceptable. I have not as yet had ye pleasure of seeing Mr. Brook, but have received from him ye Ruffles which Miss Baugh* did me ye honour to send, which I set so great a value on as determines me not to wear 'em till I return to Europe, and have ye pleasure of kissing ye fair hand that work'd 'em.

"I have ordered my attorney at Madrass to remit you 100 pounds by bill on ye Jews which I 'm informed is ye surest and best method, as ye Company don't pay till three months after sight; ye bill will accompany this, and goe I believe by ye Swallow, Capt. Spike, which triffle I beg my Dearest Mother will accept to drink my health with such of her acquaintances as have merited her esteem, for *such* I shall always deem my valuable friends. I'le write to her if possible, however if I should not be able to accomplish it, I beg you 'll let her know I am very well, and all things goes according to my desire, except ye

---

* General Lancelot Baugh left the bulk of his property to his sister who had married a Captain George Maddison.

wished for hapiness of seeing her. My best respects to your Lady, and all ye rest of your agreeable family, and believe me Dear Sir with ye highest gratitude for all favours

"Your most sincere and obliged

"Humble servant,

"JOHN DALTON.

"English Camp,

"Near Trichinopoly,

"April 29th, 1752.

"I send this to my attourney at Madrass, in order to get it conveyed per first ship, my present situation being 150 miles up ye country."

The foregoing letter was sent by the recipient to Captain Dalton's mother, who took a copy of it, and added the following memorandum to her transcript:—

"Note.—His attourney's letter was dated ye 17th of June 1752, with fresh assurance of his safety after ye battle, which was not quite at an end when my son wrote."

The two following short letters are undated, but their contents help to approximate their dates very closely.

Captain Dalton to his mother :—

" My Dearest Mother,

" This goes by Captain Clive,* a very intimate and worthy friend of mine, who I thought to have accompanied home in ye same ship, but my post here at present puts it out of my power, however you may be sure it is my full intention to leave this country next September, as my fortune is more than ever I expected, and enough my dearest Mother to keep you a chariot, and equipage in proportion, which is my greatest ambition."

The next—and unfortunately the last—letter from Captain Dalton to his mother was evidently written a few months later, when he had determined to resign his commission and return to England :—

" I remain still commanding officer of this garrison, and believe I shall continue so, as long as I stay in ye country, indeed I can't be in a better situation. When ye time comes for ye ships to sail for Europe I'll resign my commission, but should I not arrive exactly at ye time you'l by *this* expect me, I beg

* Clive's arrival in England is thus chronicled in the *Public Advertiser* of Oct. 10, 1753 :—" We hear that Captain Clive who has behaved so bravely in the East Indies is come home in the Bombay Castle Indiaman arrived at Plymouth."

you 'l not be in ye least uneasy, for forty accidents unforseen may retard me a little, while on so long a tract, and comfort yourself with the reflection that ye same all seeing Power which has hitherto been my guide will inevitably return me safe to you with ye fortune I have acquired by His blessing. At present I have little to tell you, ye French will never be quiet, tho' we often ,thrash 'em heartily, so shall only add that I am perfectly well and in good spirits, in a very advantageous post, and longing for nothing so much as to embrace my dearest-dearest Mother, for I am ever and most unalterably,

"Your most affectionate
"and dutifull son,
"JOHN DALTON."

Captain Dalton's request to be relieved from the command of Trichinopoly is thus referred to in the East India Records :—

" Fort St. George, Sept. 10th, 1753.

"Captain Dalton at Trichinopoly requests to be relieved from the command of that place. Encloses an account current of the charges of that garrison for the months of July and August, amounting to Arcot Rupees 21,727–5, whereon a Ballance of upwards of 2,000 Arcot Rupees is due to him, and advises he is under the necessity of drawing on us for more money for the charges of the next two months.

"RESOLVED — That Captain Dalton's draughts be complied with, but in regard to his request to be relieved, that Major Lawrence be desired to acquaint him we cannot immediately grant it, as he is capable from his knowledge of the country of being more serviceable than any other officer, and we expect he will continue to exert himself."

The closing remarks of the above show the high opinion the Governor and Council had of Captain Dalton's abilities and fitness for the arduous post he occupied.

It has always been a matter of wonder to those who did not know the real state of the case, that Captain Dalton should voluntarily resign his commission at the early age of twenty-eight, when he had made himself a name in Indian history, and was on the high road to rank and wealth. His letter to the Council at Fort St. George gives his real reason. It is as follows :—

"Trichinopoly,

"Sept. 30th, 1753.

"HONBLE. GENTN.,

"Major Lawrence has communicated to me a paragraph in your late letter to him, by which I find it is not agreeable to you that I am relieved from the command of this place.

"When I made application at first to Mr. Saunders on this head, I flattered myself that you would have kindly indulged me in it in consideration of the time I have been in the field, however I find to the contrary, and it will give me the greatest concern to incur the displeasure of your Honble. Board. I shall in consequence of your directions continue to take the same care I have always done of the place for two months longer, and if you judge proper to nominate the officer who is to succeed me, I shall in that time make him thoroughly acquainted, as much as lies in my power, with not only the Fort and Foible of the garrison, but likewise the nature and different interests of the people round us. At the expiration of the above-mentioned time I must request your permission to resign the service and return to Europe in the January ships, my constitution being so totally ruined that nothing but a cold climate can reinstate me. Many of my friends can inform you that it was the situation of my post only that prevented me from applying to you before for leave to go home in the ships that sail this month, but at present the great success of our arms has altered the scene much for the better, and given me the opportunity I long wished for of addressing you on this subject.

"I cannot conclude without observing to you, gentlemen, that the number of European prisoners which are now here are highly improper to be kept in this garrison where underhand schemes are so subject to be put in execution. . . . . I am with the greatest respect

"Honble. Gentlemen,

"Yr. most obedt. and very humble servant,

"JOHN DALTON."

The Governor and Council sent the following reply:—

"Fort St. George,

"Oct. 18th, 1753.

"SIR,

"We have received your letter of 30th Sept setting forth a bad state of health which nothing but a cold climate can reinstate, and your request of resigning your Commission in January to return to Europe. *The service certainly stands greatly in need of officers,* but if you continue this resolution, we have desired Major Lawrence who is on the spot to nominate such officer as he judge proper to relieve you on your resigning the command. It will be necessary you have your accounts from the time of your being there, and get them signed by the Nabob, which will prevent any disputes afterwards. . . . . We are very sensible the Nabob having so many prisoners at Trichinopoly must be a great ill-convenience in respect to the garrison and provisions, and we wish it could be removed. There are almost treble the number of the Garrison at Fort St. David already, you will therefore consult with Major Lawrence that the Nabob take the most effective measures to prevent mischief. We are, Sir,

"Your affectionate friends,

"THOMAS SAUNDERS.

"CHARLES BODDAM.

"HENRY POWNEY.

"ALEXANDER WYNCH.

"JOHN SMITH.

"CHARLES BOURCHIER."

No one can have read this narrative without perceiving what wear and tear of body and mind Captain Dalton had gone through. Added to this that he had been ten years on foreign service, five of which he had been knocking about on board a man-of-war in the Indian seas, and the last five years on continual active service in one of the most unhealthy parts of India. Clive had gone home after ten years of Indian life, with his health much shattered, and the seeds of disease sown in his constitution, which in the end led to that unhappy state of mind which caused the sad event that terminated his brilliant career.

"Glory is priceless," but there is no glory in dying of a broken down constitution or a diseased liver. Happy are those who know when to stop, and not to lose all by a too soaring ambition. It is most probable that Captain Dalton never told his mother in his letters of his broken health, and I leave it to the reader to imagine whether she ever urged him to continue in India, in order to win more renown, and increase his fortune. I do not believe a good mother would ever let ambition surmount her love for her son. I cannot give a better illustration than the mother of Lord Clive. She had a husband, six sons, and seven daughters, all living. They were very poor, and all their hopes centred on Robert Clive. When news came of his distinguished gallantry and ability in capturing Arcot with a mere handful of troops, his friends all foresaw he would attain to a high position if he continued in India, and they were anxious he should do so. Not so his mother. This is the way she speaks of it in her letter to her son, dated December, 1752:—

"I cannot express the joy yours to your father gave

to me. Your brave conduct and success which Providence has blessed you with is the talk and wonder of the public, the great joy and satisfaction of your friends, but more particularly so to me, as it gives me hopes of seeing you much sooner than I could possibly have expected. I find some of your friends wish your longer stay in India; but I earnestly entreat you will let no motive induce you, except your honour and the peace of the country require it." *

None of Mrs. Dalton's letters to her son are extant, but think you she would write in any less affectionate style than the above—she who was a widow, and had been seperated from her only child for ten long years? What good would her son's renown and fortune bring her in her old age, if he who won them was to return no more? There is still extant a letter, or part of a letter, from Mrs. Dalton to a friend, which will give the reader some idea of the depth of her love for her son:—

"Since I wrote to you last, I received an account from London that there was brought in ye Swallow† sloop of war, a parcel of valuable things for me from my son, but pursuant to my usual ill luck, they were

---

* Malcolm's *Life of Clive*, vol. I. p. 129.

† H.M.S. *Swallow*, Captain Speke, sailed for England from Madras in July, 1752.—*East India Records*.

all seized so supose I shall loose them as formerly. Alas dr. Madam is it not very cruel that I must always be deprived of these testimonys of affectionate duty from that Darling of my soul, who is ye most exemplary child that ever woman was blessed with, but I am innur'd to crosses and disappointments wch that all Gracious Power in wch. I put my trust can in his good time relieve me from, and grant me a Glorious recompense for all my sufferings, by a hapy meeting with ye dr. cause of all my anxious cares."

* * * *

Captain Dalton's departure from Trichinopoly is thus referred to by Orme:—"Captain Dalton seeing this object of the general sollicitude provided for,* and the city in all other respects out of danger, quitted the command of Trichinopoly, and some time after returned to Europe."

The following extract from Captain Dalton's Indian Journal, gives his own account of his departure:—

"Having at last with much difficulty obtained the long wish'd for leave to return to Madrass, I resigned the command of the Garrison to Capt. James Kilpatrick, who was ordered to succeed me, and November

* Referring to there being six months' provisions laid up in Trichinopoly. Orme, vol. i. p. 316.

14th, 1753, left the place with an escort of 30 soldiers and 150 Sepoys and arrived the day following at Coiladdy, where our army was in their winter quarters. The Major being much indisposed, I stayed with him 5 or 6 days and then proceeded on my journey thro' the Tanjour Dominions for the Coast. I received great civilitys in all the towns and villages of that delightful country as I passed along, the long time I had serv'd in a publick caracter having made me very well known to 'em all, and in 6 days I arrived at Davycota the southernmost settlement belonging to the Company on the coast.

"I found on my arrival there, that the French from the Garrison of Chilumbrum were besieging the fort of Pollincota, which belongs to the Nabob of Carpy. Their being masters of that place, would prove extreamly prejudicial to both St. David's and Davycota, as detachments from thence could easily intercept the Company's cloath, as well as all sorts of provisions, which we are supply'd with from the Worriarpollam country.

"As we had perfect intelligence that they had drain'd Chilumbrum of all their best men, in order to carry on this siege, I advis'd Mr. Hopkins the Chief of Davycota to write to the Governor of Fort St. David's for 100 men and a few scaling-ladders, with which I offer'd my service, to take the advantage the weakness of the garrison offer'd us. But Mr. Starke sending for answer that he coud not possibly spare such a detachment, on account of the weakness of his garrison, we contented ourselves with sending an officer with 30 soldiers and 200 Sipoys to throw themselves into Pollincota.

"The French never staid for their getting in, which they might easily have prevented, but on the first news of their approach rais'd the siege and ran away, leaving 2 12-pounders behind 'em, and all their ammunition. Lieut. Frazier who commanded our party, enter'd the fort with colours flying and was receiv'd by the inhabitants as their deliverer. After repairing the breach he mounted the enemy's two guns on the ramparts, and in several affairs which he has since had with the Chilumbrum garrison has allways defeated 'em, tho' three to one.

"While I staid at Davycota, we received the agreeable news, that since my departure from Tritchenopoly the French had made an attempt to take it by scalade,* but without success. They got in possession of the battery which goes by my name, without any opposition, owing to either the neglect or treachery of the

* "The 28th of Novr. 1753."

Jemidar of Sipoys who commanded there, and enter'd to the number of 600 French at 4 o'clock in the morning before they were perceiv'd. When they had all got up, they imagin'd the fort was their own, and turning the artillery inwards which they found on the battery they fir'd grape into the town. But they soon found they were egregiously deceiv'd in their hopes. The place they had got possession of was no more than an old gateway on the outward wall, and had no communication with the inner one, which overlook'd it by a great many foot, and they had that still to scalade, before they coud become masters of the place. The reason of my having made a battery on the gateway was in order to flank the fossé, for which purpose its projecting from the body of the place made it very convenient.

"They had made 2 other false attacks on different parts of the town, to draw the attention of the European force, while their main body made their grand effort on this. But the noise they made with their musketry, drums, and huzza's, when they had got possession of this battery, soon convinced our people that their real attack was on that side, and our European body, marching with all possible diligence, lin'd the part of the inner wall which overlook'd the battery the enemy were possessed of.

"The hot fire of musketry made by this party, join'd to the fire of 4 pieces of cannon, which from the flanks of other bastions greatly annoy'd the enemy, soon convinc'd 'em of their mistake, and a few of the bravest of 'em had resolution enough to rear 3 ladders against the inner wall. But those who first mounted being immediatly kill'd, the rest gave over the affair as impracticable, and every one endeavour'd to get himself under some shelter from the fire, which every minute became more terrible by the arrival of fresh musketeers and matchlock men from all parts of the town. When they first found their mistake, they had haul'd their ladders after 'em up the first wall in order to plant 'em against the second, which now prov'd their ruin, and left 'em no prospect of escape but by leaping a wall 30 foot high into the ditch. Finding themselves, therefore, fairly caught between the walls, they did not chuse to wait till 'twas clear day, as the garrison would then (they knew) not fire a shot in vain, but begging quarter on their knees in the most piteous manner.

"Just as the day began to dawn, 9 officers and 400 soldiers surrender'd themselves prisoners of war. 100 were found kill'd and wounded on and about the battery. And the poor remains, at the hazard of their lives, leap'd the wall and escap'd to their black army and corps de reserve which was drawn up at some distance to wait the event of the enterprize. The prisoners were immediately confin'd in the place with the rest of their countrymen, and the arms being collected amounted to 600, with one petard.

"It was with great difficulty the Sipoys and Nabob's people were restrain'd from cutting 'em all to pieces, and 'tis a pity that the humanity and mercifull disposition so natural to our nation, influenced 'em at that time to take so much pains to prevent it. For the French confess'd afterwards that they had orders to give no quarters for 4 hours had they succeeded, and had free liberty for that time to plunder the place.

"The commanding officer of the attack was excessively drunk when he was taken, as were 2 or 3 others, and their private men had no less than 9 drams each given 'em from the time they left Syringam till they planted their ladders against the fort wall. Besides every man had a small loaf of bread steeped in arrack in his pocket. The French allways use this method with their people, tho' they won't allow that it is owing to any suspicion of want of bravery to undertake any enterprize. One quarter part of such a proportion of liquor serv'd to a body of Englishmen before an action would have render'd 'em quite ungovernable."*

* Fol. 161–64.

Thus ended, in signal defeat, this attempt of the French to capture Trichinopoly. They knew that Captain Kilpatrick, the new commandant, was badly wounded, and so they hoped to take the garrison by surprise.*

In the East India Records for 1754 I find the following:—

"Fort St. George, March 4th, 1754.

"Letter from Captain Dalton read as entered hereafter, desiring leave to resign his commission and proceed to Europe on the Durrington, having delivered in all his accounts, signed by the Nabob, and requesting also a certificate of his behaviour to entitle him to his half pay in the King's Service, having been left here by Admiral Boscawen on those conditions.

"AGREED, that Captain John Dalton's resignation be accepted, that he have leave to proceed to Europe on the Durrington, and that a certificate be granted him as desired."

---

* The attack on Dalton's battery is described by Colonel Lawrence in his *Narrative*. A full account of it appeared in the *Public Advertiser* of October 28, 1754. This historical battery still bears Captain Dalton's name.

Captain Dalton's letter was as follows :—

"Fort St. David, 20th Feb. 1754.

"HONBLE. SIR AND SIRS,

"As I informed you when I applyed to be relieved from the command of the Garrison of Trichinopoly that it was my intention to resign the Hon. Co.'s Service in order to return to Europe, I must now desire your permission to do it, and that you will please to give the necessary directions to the Captain of the Durrington to receive me on board.

"I have delivered in to the Governour my account with the Nabob Annaverde Cawn,* passed and signed by him in the manner you were pleased to direct in the letter I had the honour to receive from you on that subject, and have delivered the Nabob's receipts in full from all his people that served under my command.

"As it is expected by the Lords of the Regency that the officers of His Majesty's Service left in India by Mr. Boscawen produce certificates of their behaviour in order to obtain their half pay, I must request Gentlemen that you will please to grant me such a one from your Honble. Board, as you think my behaviour

---

* Meaning Mahommed Ali, son of Anwarodean Khan, or, as the name is sometimes spelt, Annaverde Cawn.

entitles me to during the time I have had the honour to serve in your troops.

"I have now only to add my acknowledgments for the genteel treatment I have always received in your Service, and to assure you I shall always remain with the most profound respect and consideration,

"Honourable Sir and Sirs,

"Yr most obedient

"And very Humble servant,

"J. DALTON."

"To the Honble. Thos. Saunders, Esq.,

"Presidt. and Govr., &c., Council of

"Fort St. George."

I find this entry among the accounts, under date of March 9, 1754:—

"The Secretary pays in 30 Pagodas on account of Capt. John Dalton for permission of passage to Europe on the Durrington."

The "Durrington" sailed for England on March 10, as shown by this entry in the Records:—

"Hon. Co.'s ship 'Durrington,' Richard Drake, for England."

Extract from Captain Dalton's *Journal*:—

"Having taken my passage on board the Durrington, Indiaman, for Europe, I resigned my Commission to the Governor and Council the 1st March, 1754, who were pleased to return me thanks for my services, and on the 10th of the same month we sailed from Madrass Road."

CHAPTER XIII.

CONCLUSION.

And thus the dying veteran spake:
"My son! I leave to thee a prize—
The sword of Bunker Hill."

"MADE the Scilly Isles off Land's End, 30th September 1754. Total from the time of our leaving St. David's in India to our making the Scilly Islands off the Land's End of England, 14,520, run by the logg, in miles. The true distance in miles, 13,917."

Thus ends Captain Dalton's *Journal*. The "Durrington" arrived at Portsmouth on October 2,* and so, after an absence of ten and a half eventful years, John Dalton returned to the port he had sailed from in H.M.S. "Preston." He had left Portsmouth as a subaltern, with little, if anything, beyond his pay to

---

* *Public Advertiser*, Oct 3, 1754.

support him. He returned there with a fortune of £10,000, and a very fair share of military fame. Excepting the "thanks" of the Governor and Members of Council, Captain Dalton received no other honours from the East India Company for his important services. In that early stage of their existence the Company did not generally give pensions, bonuses, or decorations. In these days one quarter of Captain Dalton's services would have been recognised by promotion and other honours; but as he amassed a good fortune in India he may be said to have derived the most solid advantages from his Indian service. The Nabob of Arcot behaved very generously to the defender of Trichinopoly, and, besides other presents, presented Dalton with a sword*—a good cut-and-thrust weapon, which would have cheered the heart of the most stalwart Highland chieftain out on the war-path in the "forty-five." This sword has been as much

---

* This sword, which has a red velvet covered scabbard with silver mountings, is preserved at Langton Hall. The Dorsetshire Regiment (old 39th) possess a remembrance of the Nabob of Arcot in the shape of a handsome silver-mounted drum-major's cane which Mahommed Ali presented to the corps in 1757, with the following device and inscription thereon:—

Device—An Elephant, with motto, "Primus in Indis," Plassey, 1757.

Inscription—" Nabob of Bengal overturned by the 39th Regiment and the Company's troops the 22nd September, 1757."

cherished by Captain Dalton's descendants as the sword referred to in the American poem—the sword of Bunker Hill!

A century and a quarter have passed since John Dalton's return home, after an absence of nearly eleven years, but it is pleasant to picture the joyful meeting between the long-parted mother and son. It is only a picture which a romantic fancy can depict, as there is nothing left on record to tell us of it. I believe his mother to have resided at Kendal since she lost her husband. And her son's visits there are borne testimony to by two original portraits of him by George Romney, who resided some time at Kendal before proceeding to London in 1762, and painted portraits at two and a half guineas per head, which price he raised to five guineas when he went to London.

In the "Army List," published by authority in 1755, the name of John Dalton appears, under the following head:—

"Half-Pay. Twelve Independent Companies from the East Indies under Admiral Boscawen."

"1st Lieutenants:—

"Colin Campbell,
"Lauchlan McPherson,
"Dugald Campbell,
"John Dalton,
"Mathew Walker."

His half-pay as 1st Lieutenant was 2s. 4d. per day. In the following year his name disappeared from the above list. Whether he voluntarily resigned his half-pay on his marriage, or commuted it, does not appear; but I think it most likely that he was allowed to commute his pension for a sum of money down, as is often done in the present day, and always gives satisfaction to the recipient at the time, whatever it may do afterwards.

We now come to what may be termed the most important domestic event in Captain Dalton's life. This was his engagement, and subsequent marriage to, the second daughter of Sir John Wray,* Bart., of Glentworth, Lincolnshire, and Sleningford Park, Yorkshire. There is a tinge of romance about his meeting with this lady which he himself used to love to tell to his family in after years, and relate how Fortune gave him the greatest prize which she could possibly have bestowed. This was how it happened. Being one evening at the village inn at Greenhammerton, near York, there arrived late in the evening in their chariot the widowed Lady Wray and her daughters. There

---

* Twelfth Bart. of Glentworth. He married, March 4, 1727–8, Frances Norcliffe, daughter, and eventual heir, of Colonel Fairfax Norcliffe, of Langton.

was no sitting-room free for them, so Captain Dalton immediately sent them word he would vacate his, and retire to his bedroom. They could do no less than request him to stay and sup with them, which he did, and hence arose the attachment to Miss Isabella Wray, the second daughter, which ended in their marriage on March 7, 1756, in Ripon Minster.*

* * * * *

In 1769 Mrs. James Dalton died at Kendal, and was buried in the parish church, where is still to be seen a small brass inscribed with the name of "Elizabeth Dalton, widow of Captain James Dalton of the 6th Regiment, who departed this life the 11 of July 1769." She lived to see her son surrounded by all those blessings which tend to make a good man happy; and this happiness threw a bright reflection over the declining years of one who had been sorely tried in life's rough journey.

Six children were born to John and Isabella Dalton —three sons and three daughters. Of these, five lived to maturity; the other, a daughter, died an infant. The eldest son entered the army at an early age,

---

* "March 7, 1756, John Dalton, Esq., of the parish of Hauxwell, and Isabella Wray, of this parish." — Marriage registers, Ripon Minster.

and in 1780 attained the rank of captain in the 11th Light Dragoons. When quartered in Scotland, as a subaltern, Thomas Norcliffe Dalton received much kindness from the Earl and Countess of Northesk. The former had renewed his old acquaintance and friendship with Captain Dalton, who had served three years as a Marine officer on board the Earl's ship, the "Preston." There is a letter still extant from Anne Countess of Northesk to the Lady Torpichen,* Bristol Street, Edinburgh, speaking of the great desire her Lord and herself had to show some civility to Captain Dalton; how little they could do to entertain a young man; that at Hopetoun House he would see the best that Scotland affords; that Lord Hope† will be very glad to see him. "I am sure," continues her Ladyship, "it has hurt both my Lord and I greatly that we cannot show Mr. Dalton how much we esteem his parents in him, and the old kindness and goodwill that was between his father and him we would wish to be continued by generation between their children and ours. I trust to your Ladyship's

---

* Widow of the 8th Baron Torpichen.

† James Lord Hope succeeded as 3rd Earl of Hopetoun in 1781. He married, in 1766, Elizabeth, eldest daughter of Admiral the Earl of Northesk.

goodness to make this letter acceptable to Mr. Dalton; and when next you write to Mrs. Dalton, will your Ladyship forgive me to beg you will take the trouble of offering our best and most sincere good wishes for their health and happiness and that of their family. The fine little girl I saw with Lady Wrey (*sic*) will now be a woman almost." *

The "fine little girl" referred to in Lady Northesk's letter, was either Captain Dalton's elder daughter, Frances Elizabeth, who married, in 1778, William Garforth, Esq., of Wiganthorpe, Yorkshire, or his equally handsome younger daughter, Isabella, who married, in 1787, George Baker, Esq., of Elemore, Durham. The latter daughter had the honour of being Lord Clive's god-daughter, as the following entry in the Dalton family Bible records:—

"Isabella, the third daughter,† born December 8, 1763, on Thursday at half an hour before two in the afternoon. Gossips: Lady Vanburgh, Mrs. Arthington and the Rt. Honble. Lord Clive."

In 1763 Lord Clive was in England, and the two old friends and companions in arms doubtless met on several occasions. Had Lord Clive been spared a few

---

* Undated, but written before 29th May, 1780.

† The second daughter died an infant.

years longer to his friends, he would have had every reason to feel proud of his god-daughter.

Were this not a biography, I would now close my narrative with the Nabob of Arcot's exclamation of—

"WHAT CAN I SAY MORE?"

but the laws of biography compel me to go on to the very end.

After twenty-four years of happy married life, Captain Dalton had the misfortune to lose his wife, and after his daughter Isabella's marriage he, in 1787, resided by himself at Sleningford, near Ripon, in the old Wray mansion, which he had purchased from his brother-in-law, Sir Cecil Wray. He lived to see his eldest son—who made an advantageous marriage in 1784—succeed to the Norcliffe estate in 1807 * on the death of his maternal aunt, Lady Norcliffe of Langton. He lived to see his second son and namesake attain the rank of major and brevet lieutenant-colonel in the 4th Light Dragoons, after having served for a short time in North America under his father-in-law General Prescott, to whom the young John Dalton acted as aide-de-camp. He lived to see his youngest son,

* On succeeding to the Norcliffe estates, Captain Thomas Dalton assumed by royal license the name and arms of Norcliffe.—*London Gazette.*

James,* enter the church, and make a very happy and advantageous marriage. And in the happiness and prosperity of his sons and daughters, the old veteran enjoyed a bright and happy old age. His martial spirit descended on his children to the third and fourth generation. In the Peninsular war, the only son † of the old veteran's eldest son highly distinguished himself as a lieutenant in the 4th Dragoons, at the battle of Salamanca, where he was badly wounded; and another grandson ‡ (the eldest son of Lieutenant-Colonel Dalton) also took part in several of the hard-fought battles of that great war.

On July 11, 1811, the forty-second anniversary of his beloved mother's death, the spirit of the single-minded and brave old soldier passed

"From life across the sea of death—home."

---

* He was Rector of Croft, Yorkshire, for over thirty years.

† Afterwards Major-General Norcliffe Norcliffe, K.H., of Langton.

‡ Captain John Dalton of the 4th Dragoons, who eventually inherited Sleningford, and the Lincolnshire estates of the extinct Baronets Wray. He was father of the gallant Major Thomas Norcliffe Dalton, of the 49th Regiment, who was killed at the battle of Inkermann.

APPENDIX.

APPENDIX.

Commissions, 1716–20. Irish Establishment.

James Dalton, Gent. — A commission dated the 3rd day of July 1718, and signed as above (*i.e.* by the Irish Council) to be Ensign of the Company whereof John Murray, Esq., is Captain, in the room of John Cottrell, in the Regiment of Foot commanded by the Hon. Colonel Robert Dormer.

(From the Record Office, Dublin.)

Marching Orders.

An order dated July 11, 1719, for Colonel Dormer's Regiment of Foot to march from Dublin to Limerick . . . . to reach Limerick barracks August 4.

(Record Office, Dublin.)

Miscellaneous Entries.

Several companies of Dormer's Regiment at Kinsale in November 1723. Four companies at Waterford in February 1725. Head-quarters of the Regiment in Dublin in August 1725. One company at Palmerstown, in County Dublin, autumn of 1725.

(Record Office, Dublin.)

List of Officers in Dormer's Regiment of Foot, September, 1727 :—

Field Officers and Captains.	Lieutenants.	Ensigns.
James Dormer, Col.	Elias Landy, Capt.-Lieut.	Wm. Jenkins.
John Murray, Lt.-Col.	C. Nelson.	Ancketell Moutray.
John Cotterell, Major	Albert De Brisay.	Thomas Freeman.
Richard Miller, Captain	Abraham Hunt.	Francis Marcier.
Nathaniel Mitchell	Wm. Goodricke.	Wm. Burrard.
Arthur Brereton	George Bell.	Fras. Lestrange.
Robert Saunders	John Swetenham.	Oliver Walsh.
Frederick Gore	James McGee.	Lancelot Baugh.
Edward Southwell	John Galt.	Davis Bayley.
Philip Beard	James Dalton. } Grenadiers.	
	Henry Jolly. } Grenadiers.	

Staff Officers.

John Johnston, Chaplain.
Francis Marcier, Adjutant.
George Bell, Surgeon.

(Record Office, Dublin.)

Dublin Journal, May 7, 1726.

The Right Hon. the Earl of Cavan has disposed of the Lieutenant-Colonelcy of Brigadier Dormer's Regiment to Major Murray.

Embarkation Orders.

Colonel Guise's Regiment of Foot (late Dormer's) to sail from Donaghadee, County Down, June 30, 1739.

(Record Office, Dublin.)

Army List, 1740, in the Royal United Service Library, Whitehall Yard, S.W., gives the following list of Officers in Brigadier Guise's Regiment of Foot:—

	Date of present commission.
Brigadier-General—	
John Guize,* as Colonel - -	1 Nov. 1738.
Lieutenant-Colonel—	
John Murray - - - -	6 July, 1726.
Major—	
Nathaniel Mitchell - - -	19 Jan. 1739–40.
Captains—	
Richard Miller - - - -	6 Feb. 1718–19.
Arthur Brereton - - -	29 Aug. 1721.
Frederick Gore - - -	5 April, 1726.
James Hamilton - - -	11 Jan. 1728–9.
Henry Southwell - - -	28 Jan. 1735–6.
Abraham Hunt† - - -	14 Aug. 1738.
George Bell† - - - -	19 Jan. 1739–40.
Captain-Lieutenant—	
James Dalton† - - - -	Ditto.
Lieutenants—	
John Swetenham - - -	29 Aug. 1721.
Abraham Hamilton - - -	11 Jan. 1728–9.
Davis Baylie† - - - -	25 Jan. 1729–30.
John Boitoux† - - - -	19 Aug. 1731.
Francis Mercier† - - -	16 April, 1753.
Ank. Montray - - - -	3 July, 1733.
Oliver Walsh† - - - -	26 Aug. 1737.
John Lucas† - - - -	31 Jan. 1737–8.
George Holwell - - -	14 Aug. 1738.
Alex. Murray - - - -	19 Jan. 1739–40.

* Many years Governor of Berwick; he died a General in June, 1765.

† Died on active service in the West Indies between March 8 and May 18, 1742. Administration of the effects of Captain Abraham Hunt, "who died in Jamaica," formerly of Pontvine (?) N.B., was granted October 26, 1743, to his widow, Margaret Hunt.

Ensigns—	Date of present commission.
James Murray - - - -	25 Jan. 1739–40.
Thomas Coote - - - -	16 April, 1733.
Thomas Garaway* - - -	25 April, 1733.
George Willan - - -	3 July, 1733.
William Richardson - - -	26 March, 1737.
Edward Wilson - - -	27 Aug. 1737.
Benjamin Foyster* - - -	31 Jan. 1737–8.
Tomkins Powell* - - -	4 Feb. 1738–9.
Sir William Maxwell - -	3 Feb. 1734–5.

Establishment of Pensions for Widows of Officers.

List for July 1743 in the Public Record Office, London: Guise's Regiment.

Names of Widows.	Quality of their husbands.	Pension per ann.
Mary Collyer -	Captain - -	£26
Anne Duval -	Lieutenant -	20
Elizabeth Warner	Do. -	20
Mary Goodricke -	Do. -	20
Ellen Beard -	Captain - -	26
Ann Landy -	Captain-Lieut. -	20
Elizabeth McGee -	Lieutenant -	20
Anne Saunders -	Captain - -	26
Catherine Willan -	Ensign - -	16
Mary Mercier -	Lieutenant -	20
Ann Bailie - -	Do. -	20
Margaret Hunt -	Captain - -	26
Elizabeth Dalton -	Do. -	26†

* Died on active service in the West Indies between March 8 and May 18, 1742.

† It will be seen from this pension that James Dalton was a Captain and not a Captain-Lieutenant in the regiment when he died. The pension for a captain-lieutenant's widow *was only* £20 *a year*. It appears from a later list of pensions in the Public Record Office, London, that John Boitoux was Captain-Lieutenant of Guise's Regiment at his death in the spring of 1742, and his widow received a pension of £20 per annum.

Captain Dalton's Manuscript at Langton Hall.

Year.	Subject.	Page in the MS.	Page in Orme, 3rd ed., vol. i.
1743.	Siege of Pondicherry - -	1	79–81
1749.	Death of Nabob of Arcot - -	2	127, 128
1750.	Trivadi - - - - - -	2	167
	Dupleix - - - - - -	3	130–132
1750.	April. Lawrence returns to Fort St. David - - - - -	3	146
	The Soubah to Arcot - -	3	171
	Trivendiparam - - - -	4–9	148–150
1750.	Oct. Lawrence goes to England	10	167
	Chunda Sahib - - -	10	118, 119
$175\frac{0}{1}$.	March 1. Embassy - - -	14	138
	March 24. Commander, French Deserters, and Retreat - -	15, 16	140
	Marzafa Jung surrenders -	—	141
	Conspiracy. The Nabob - -	19	145
1750.	Dec. 20, 21. Would take no warning - - - - -	20, 21	155, 156
1751.	May 21. Verdachelem - -	23	171
1751.	June 19. Volcondah - -	24–29	171–74
	Plan of the Battlefield of Utatoor - - - - - -	30, 31	174, 175
	Plan of the Battlefield.		
1751.	July 13. Advanced Guard -	32, 34	175, 176
	[Compare this paragraph with Orme.]		
	Retreat on Trichinopoly - -	34	177–189
1751.	Aug. Coiladdy - - -	38	180, 181
	Siege of Trichinopoly lasted three months - - -	39	200
	Innis Khan - - - - -	48–51	204, 205
	Jackalls and Arcot - - -		206
	Clive at Arcot - - - -	41, 45, 58	
$175\frac{1}{2}$.	Trusler and Cope's Expedition and Captain Dalton's - -	52, 55, 58	206, 207
	Trichinopoly - - - - -	59	207

Year.	Subject.	Page in the MS.	Page in Orme, 3rd ed., vol. i.
1752.	March 15. Lawrence arrives -		213
1752.	March 27. Coiladdy - -	61	214
	Action. Lawrence and Dalton -	62–64	214–16
1752.	April 1. Elmiserum - - -	65, 66	218
	Clive - - - - - -	65, 66	220, 221
	Surprise - - - - -	66, 67, 71	223, 224, 226
1752.	May 10. Wootatoor - - -	71, 72	226, 227
1752.	May 12. Captain Dalton serves as a Volunteer under Clive -	74	223
	Pitchunda Pagoda - - Dalton is hurt by a gun bursting, and is on crutches for a month - - -	75, 76	228, 229 230
	Indian Horse came over - -	77	231
	D'Auteuil defeated at Volcondah	78–80	233, 235
	Surrender of Syringam - -	82, 82, 84	239, 240
1752.	June 15. Captain Dalton appointed Commandant of Trichinopoly. The Nabob about surrendering Trichinopoly - - -	86	244
1752.	Interview with Morari Row -	88	245, 246
	Gingee. Major Kincer - -	91–93	253, 254
	Action at Villanore - - -	94, 95	255–57
1752.	Dec. 1. Attempt to shoot Dalton	97–100	258
	Poverio - - - - - -	100–102	258–60
	Skirmish before Trivady - -	110–15	
1752.	Dec. 23. Night Attack - -	120–22	
	Entrenchment and Disaster -	123	270, 271
	Dismissal of 700 Mysoreans -	126	271
	Velore Pagoda - - -	126	272
	Night Action - - - - -	127	272
	Scarcity of Provisions - -	128	273
	Scarcity of Provisions - -	129	280
	Defeat of the Enemy and Retreat - - - - - -	129–32	282, 283

Year.	Subject.	Page in the MS.	Page in Orme, 3rd ed., vol. i.
1753.	April 29. Action - - - -	132, 133	283–85
	Unsuccessful attempt to get Provisions from Polygar -	134	287
	Statement of French and English Forces - - - - -	134	289–93
1753.	June 16. Action. Loss of the "Five Rocks" - - -	135–40	
	Fall of Trivady - -	141	285–87
	The Nabob threatened by his own Troops - - - -	142	294
1753.	June 20. Lawrence leaves Trichinopoly - -	142–47	296–302
	Dalton mines Weyconda and Warriore - - -		
	Episode of De Cattans -		
1753.	July 28. Sally - -		
1753.	Aug. 25. Action. Lawrence beats the French - -	148, 149	
	Morarow's army arrives, but the French dared not attack -	149, 150	304–306
1753.	Sept. 17. Action - - - -	150–58	307–16
	Capt. Dalton wishes to return to Europe. The Nabob is unwilling. Lawrence refuses -	159	316
	Capt. Dalton's successor, Capt. James Kilpatrick, named -	160	
1753.	Nov. 14. Dalton leaves Trichinopoly - - - - -		316
	Dalton volunteers to relieve Pollincota - - - -	161	326
1753.	Nov. 28. News of the French attack on Dalton's Battery -	161–63	320–24
	Lawrence returned to Trichinopoly - - - - -	164	324
1754.	Feb. 26. Disastrous Action -	165, 166	344, 345

EXTRACT from CAPTAIN DALTON'S MS. JOURNAL with the parallel passage in ORME.

Dalton's Journal. Fos. 34–5.	*Orme's History.* Edit. 1775, pp. 176-7.
"The enemy's whole army by following us so close all the way, were led within a very little distance of the battalion drawn up with 8 pieces of cannon in their front, which they found themselves expos'd to as soon as we formed in a line with the rest. They for some time made a halt and endeavour'd to keep their ground sheltered by the rocks and stones, but our artillery officer ply'd them so warmly with his guns that they found it impossible to stay, and in quitting their cover to run off suffer'd very much as long as our cannon could reach them, and left all their dead on the spot. The French never appear'd until the affair was over, and then came and encamp'd on the ground I had quitted with the advanced guard. Their black camp extending itself along the foot of the mountains, the French pitched their tents in the little tope of green trees, mark'd on the plan, by which means the advanc'd guard from our camp and theirs were within musket shot of each other.	"The enemy following them were insensibly led within a small distance of the whole force now united with eight pieces of cannon in front; they at first appeared determined to stand their ground and bring on a general action; but finding themselves severely galled by the artillery, which together with the whole line advanced upon them, they gave way and lost 300 men before they got out of cannon-shot: their cannon were ill served and did but little damage, and the French battalion never appeared until the firing ceased, when they were discovered taking possession of the village, in the rear of which the rest of the army likewise pitched their tents.
"We had found in this late action enough to do to repulse their numerous black army, but now that they were join'd by a number of Europeans at least equal to ours, and a regular train of artillery, the sight of so superior a force now become so near neighbours to us, made us resolve not to wait the next day, when	"Altho' the post in the streights was deemed defensible, it was feared from the great superiority of Chunda Saheb's cavalry and Sepoys that he would detach a body of men, and post it between the camp and Trichinopoly, from which city the army drew all its provisions across the two largest rivers in the Carnatic. From this

Dalton's Journal—cont.

'twas probable they would renew the attack with their united force, so we decamp'd silently in the night, and marching through Wootatoor village, took the garrison out of the fort with us, as the place was not tenable, and then proceeded on our march for Tritchenopoly. We never halted till 2 o'clock the next day, when we arriv'd on the banks of the great Coleroon river about 3 or 4 miles from that place, with our poor people almost jaded to death. 'Tis astonishing how they were able to perform a march of 18 hours without refreshment, after the fatigue they had undergone in the action which kept them under arms from morning to 4 in the evening, and we march'd off at 8 o'clock at night, yet they did it with great cheerfulness considering our situation at the time."

Orme's History—cont.

apprehension it was determined to retreat without delay, and the army decamped silently in the night; they never halted till two the next day, fatigued to excess with a march of eighteen hours, performed without rest in the hottest season of this sultry climate, and after the fatigue they had endured in the action of the preceding day."